Panorama

An advanced course of English for study and examinations

Ray Williams

Longman

LONGMAN GROUP UK LIMITED
Longman House, Burnt Mill, Harlow,
Essex CM20 2JE, England
and Associated Companies throughout the world.

© Longman Group Limited 1982

First published 1982
Seventh impression 1989

ISBN 0-582-55358-X

ACKNOWLEDGEMENTS

We are grateful to the following for permission to reproduce copyright material:
The Controller of Her Majesty's Stationery Office for extracts from *Our Changing Climate* by T. Williamson, published by H.M.S.O. 1977; Intermediate Technology Publications Ltd. for an extract adapted from the article 'The Cassava Grinder' in the journal of *Appropriate Technology*. Reproduced by kind permission; Frederick Muller Ltd. for an extract from *Small Is Beautiful* by E.F. Schumacher; Wayland Publishers Ltd. for extracts adapted from *Waste-Age Man* by J. Holliman (Wayland 1974) and *The Human Multitude* by R. McDougall (Wayland 1975). For adapted extracts from *Living in the Environment, Concepts, Problems, and Alternatives* by G. Tyler Miller, Jr. © 1975 by Wadsworth Publishing Company, Inc., Belmont, California 94002. Reprinted by permission of the publisher.

Centre for World Development Education for page 44; The Engineer for page 76; Intermediate Technology Publications Ltd., for page 52; The Limits to Growth: *A report for the Club of Rome's Project on the Predicament of Mankind*, by Donella H. Meadows, Dennis L. Meadows, Jørgen Randers, William W. Behrens 111. A Potomac Associates book, published by Universe Books, N.Y., 1972. Graphics by Potomac Associates for page 60; Volunteers In Technical Assistance for page 51; Wadsworth Publishing Company, Inc., Belmont, California 94002 for pages.7 (bottom), 22 (bottom) (Modified after Combustion Power Company, Sweden), 23, 25 (right), 30 (Source: UN Food and Agricultural Organisation, *The State of Food and Agriculture*), 32, 34 (Source: UN Food and Agricultural Organisation, *Fisheries Yearbook*), 36 (top) (Source: National Academy of Sciences 1969b), 36 (bottom), 58 (bottom), 61 (Modified after Lambert & Reid 1970), 64, 73 (bottom), 74, 75, 78 (left), 78 (right) (Source: United Nations), 83 (Source of data: Murozumi et al. 1965, 1969), tables page 84 (top), 84 (bottom) (Source: National Commission on the Causes and Prevention of Violence), page 85 (Modified after Wolman and Lockwood 1969), table page 88 (bottom) (Source: Landsburg 1970), pages 94 (top) (Data from Callendar 1958, Matcha 1971), 94 (bottom), and 98.

We have been unable to trace the copyright holder of the material on pages 70 and 73 (top), and would be grateful for any information that would enable us to do so.

Illustrations by Illustra.

Produced by Longman Singapore Publishers Pte Ltd
Printed in Singapore

Contents

Introduction

Study Reading

Annual report on Spaceship Earth

Passengers of Earth:

We are on a spaceship – Spaceship Earth. It is time for you to hear the annual report on the state of our ship. As you know, we are hurtling[1] through space at about 107 000 km/hr on a fixed course. Although we can never return to home base to take on new supplies, the ship has a
5 marvellous and intricate life-support system. The system uses solar energy to recycle[2] the chemicals needed to provide a reasonable number of us with adequate water, air and food.

Let me briefly summarise the state of our passengers and our life-support
10 system. There are about 4 billion of us on board, with more than 150 nations occupying various sections of the craft[3]. About 25% of you have inherited the good to luxurious quarters in the tourist and first-class sections, and you have used approximately 80% of all resources[4] available this past year. In fact, most of the North Americans have the more lavish
15 quarters. Even though they represent only about 5% of our total population, they have consumed[5] about 35% of this year's resources.

I am sad to say that things have not really improved this year for the 75% of our passengers travelling in the hold[6]. Over one third[7] of you are suffering from hunger, malnutrition[8], or both, and three quarters[7] of you do
20 not have adequate water or shelter. These numbers[9] will certainly rise as your soaring[10] population growth wipes out any gains in food supply and economic development.

Discussion questions

A The text compares the Earth to a spaceship. In what ways is this a valid (sensible) comparison, and in what ways is it not?

B *Why* can we ... never return to home base to take on new supplies'?

C The text refers to the Earth's *life-support system*. Which of these is a system:

the heart
education
a knife
a supermarket
a bottle of ink
all the railway stations and tracks in a country

D Why does the text address the reader in this personal way – 'Passengers of Earth ... we ... you', etc.?

Study reading techniques

Study reading means reading in order to extract important information from a text, recording that information (probably in note-form), and using it for study or professional purposes. Each Study Reading section in this book contains two types of question. Discussion questions – **A, B, C**... – are to check your general understanding and to provoke discussion. Study Reading questions – [1,2,3]... – practice a variety of study reading techniques. This unit introduces those techniques.

Contextual guessing of unfamiliar words

A technique for working out the meaning of an unfamiliar word is to examine the *context* in which the word appears, i.e. the words and sentences before and after the unfamiliar word. For example,

[1] *hurtling*: What is the context of *hurtling*? The *Earth* is hurtling. It is hurtling at about *107 000 km/hr* (i.e. very, very fast). From the context, then, *hurtling* suggests 'moving extremely fast'. Similarly,

[4] *resources*: The context tells us that resources are *used* in some way, and that *the North Americans use a disproportionate share* of the Earth's resources. *What* do the North Americans use a disproportionate share of? Answer – energy, food, paper, etc. These are examples of resources.

Consider the contexts of the following words, in order to make an intelligent guess as to their meanings:

[5] *consumed*   [6] *the hold*   [10] *soaring*

Word analysis

Some words contain 'word parts', which contribute to the meaning of the word as a whole. Therefore, another technique for working out the meaning of an unfamiliar word is to see whether the word contains one or more 'word parts'. Consider the word *inaudible*:

PREFIX	ROOT	SUFFIX
in	aud	ible
not	hear	able to be

(=)

Word analysis therefore shows us that *inaudible* means 'cannot be heard'. To decide on the meanings of word parts, it is often useful to think of other words containing the same part, with which you are more familiar. Use the technique of word analysis to work out the meanings of:

[2] *recycle* (Think of *re*vise, bi*cycle*.)

[8] *malnutrition* (Think of a *mal*ignant growth such as cancer, or the *mal*function of a machine. Think also of *nutritious* food.)

Linking back devices

A *linking back device* is a way of relating to something that has previously been mentioned in the text in full. An example in paragraph 2, line 15 is *they*, which links back to *most of the North Americans*. An efficient reader will not only recognise that a word or phrase *is* a linking back device, but also identify what it links back to. What do the following link back to?

[3] *the craft* (*which* craft?)

[7] *Over one third...three quarters* (of how many?)

[9] *These numbers* (*which* numbers?)

However, the overpopulation of the hold in relation to available food is only part of the problem[11]. There is a second type of overpopulation that
25 is even more serious, because it threatens our entire life-support system. This type is occurring in the tourist and first-class sections. These sections are overpopulated in relation to the level of resource consumption and the resultant pollution of our environment. For example[12], the average North American has about 25 to 50 times as much impact on our
30 life-support system as each passenger travelling in the hold, because the North American consumes 25 to 50 times as much of our resources, and causes 25 to 50 times as much pollution. In this sense, then[13], the North American section is the most overpopulated one on the ship.

In addition to these matters, I am concerned at the lack of co-operation
35 and the continued fighting among some groups, which can destroy many, if not all, of us. Only about 10% of you are American and Russian, but your powerful weapons and your unceasing threats to build even more destructive ones must concern each of us[14]

Passengers of Earth: we are now entering the early stages of our first
40 major spaceship crisis – an interlocking crisis of over-population, pollution, resource depletion, and the danger of mass destruction by intergroup warfare. Our most thoughtful experts agree that the situation on this ship is serious, but certainly not hopeless. On the contrary[15], they feel that it is well within man's ability to learn how to control our popula-
45 tion growth, pollution, and resource consumption, and to learn how to live together in co-operation and peace. But we have only about 30 to 50 years to deal with these matters, and we must begin now.

In each unit of this book we shall investigate a particular environmental problem facing Spaceship Earth. You are invited to think seriously about these important issues, to relate them to life in your own country, and to consider what you personally can do about these problems.

Discussion questions

E   In the sense of impact on our life-support system, how much more overpopulated is the USA (approx. 215 million) than China (approx. 970 million)?

F   '...the continued fighting among some groups...can destroy many, if not all, of us.' What does this mean? In what way can this fighting destroy *all* of us?

G   Why does the text suggest that we have only 30 to 50 years to deal with our spaceship crisis? What do you think might happen if we have not dealt with it by then?

Signpost words
A text is not a series of unconnected clauses and sentences one after the other, like cars on a road. Instead, clauses and sentences *cohere* (stick together), like railway carriages. And one group of words that help them cohere are called *signpost words*. Consider: *The world's oil resources will probably be exhausted by the middle of the 21st century, but...* We do not yet know the exact words that are to come, but the signpost word *but* tells us what *type* of information to expect. The function of a signpost
4   word, then, is to tell the reader what type of information comes next.

Introduction

The following are some of the more common signpost words used in formal writing. The symbols beside them suggest how they connect information before and after. Suggest a suitable sentence to follow each signpost word.

however warns the reader that the line of reasoning is about to change course, e.g. *Many people believe that nuclear power will solve our energy problems. However, ...*

in fact introduces specific information to support the wider, more general information just given, e.g. *There is always the possibility of a major accident with nuclear power. In fact, ...*

on the contrary reinforces and expands the information just given. (The information in the sentence before *on the contrary* is always negative; the information after *on the contrary* is positive.) e.g. *We have not yet exhausted the amount of land that can support human life. On the contrary, ...*

moreover develops the ideas, facts or reasons already given, by presenting additional ones, e.g. *Scientists and engineers are already draining forest swampland. Moreover, ...*

as a result introduces the result of the information or argument given in the preceding sentence(s), e.g. *Improved varieties of rice and grain are being developed. As a result, ...*

e.g. *for example* gives an example of something just mentioned, e.g. *Many countries have pollution problems. For example, ...*

in brief summarises the preceding reasoning, e.g. *The Earth is suffering from overpopulation, resource depletion, pollution, and the danger of intergroup warfare. In brief, ...*

meanwhile introduces a reference to an event that takes place during the time that the preceding event takes place, e.g. *In the last ten years, oil consumption has more than doubled. Meanwhile, ...*

therefore introduces the reason why the preceding statement, data, etc. was presented, e.g. *The sea provides us with food. Therefore, ...*

of course reminds the reader of something he already knows or assumes, in case he has forgotten or does not fully understand, e.g. *Scientists are developing varieties of 'artificial' food. Of course, ...*

i.e. *in other words* restates the information just given, but in a different and simpler form, so as to help the reader understand, e.g. *For all practical purposes, the Earth is a closed system. In other words, ...*

in conclusion tells the reader that he has reached the end of the line of reasoning, e.g. *In conclusion, signpost words ...*

(Which five of the above symbols are in standard use?)

The following signpost words are each very similar in meaning to one of those above. Copy the list, and indicate their function by drawing the appropriate symbol against each one.

naturally	to sum up	in the meantime	thus
nevertheless	hence	to summarise	..., then, ...
in addition	for instance	obviously	consequently
so	furthermore	additionally	accordingly
that is (to say)	in short	yet	nonetheless

5

The text on p. 4 includes the following three signpost words. Summarise the information before and after, and draw the appropriate symbol to show the relationship between the two types of information in each case.

12 ... ☐ ...   13 . ... ☐ ...   15 ☐

Sentence skeletons

For full comprehension of a sentence, you must be able to identify the basic skeleton of that sentence. In other words, you must at least be able to identify the subject and principal verb. This is easy in simple sentences such as:

> *The ocean provides food.*

But books and articles often contain long sentences beginning with subjects that consist of several words. Such *extended subjects* contain other nouns in addition to the principal noun, and also verbs, e.g.

> The <u>pollution</u> of our environment by industrial waste, pesticides, solid wastes and oil spills, all of which have serious and lasting effects, is worrying many scientists.

In this sentence, the words underlined form the extended subject, and the word double-underlined (*pollution*) is the principal noun within the extended subject. The principal verb is *is worrying*.

If you have difficulty understanding a long sentence, the reason is probably because it contains an extended subject. You should therefore:

FIRST,   search for the principal verb – it will usually appear late in the sentence.

SECOND,   ask yourself '*what* verbs . . .?' e.g. '*What* is worrying many scientists?' Answer – *pollution*. The answer to this question is the principal noun, which usually occurs early in extended subjects.

Two sentences in the text contain extended subjects:

11 *What* is only part of the problem? (Answer in one word, i.e. give the principal noun of the extended subject.)

14 *What* must concern each of us? (Answer in two words, i.e. give the two principal nouns of the extended subject.)

Text structure

Every text has a *structure*. The purpose of this structure is to enable the reader to understand the text's *meaning* so that he can move smoothly from one point to the next. Copy and complete the following flowchart, to show the structure of the last paragraph:

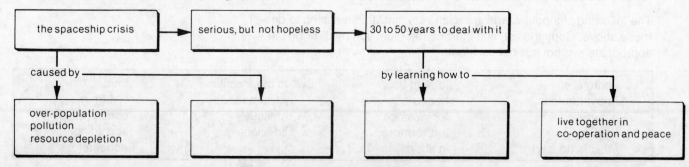

Making Notes from a Talk

You will hear a short talk about 'J' curves and their consequences. As you listen to the talk, study the graphs below, and copy and complete the tables.

Exponential growth resulting from doubling a page of a book	
NUMBERS OF DOUBLINGS	THICKNESS
0	0·1 mm
1	0·2 mm
2	0·4 mm
3	
4	
5	
8	
12	
20	
35	
42	(i.e.)
50	(i.e.)

a 'J' curve

Human population increase		
Net birth-rate:	per minute =	per day
−Net death-rate:	per minute =	per day
∴ Net population increase	=	per day
	=	per week
	=	p.a.

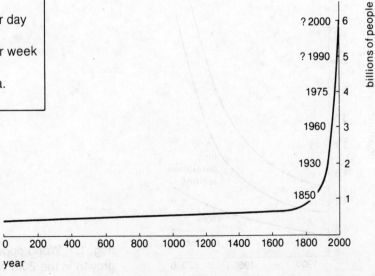

The world's population growth

Unit one: Population

Study Reading

Population growth

The human population has grown dramatically[1] this century. As Fig. 1.1 shows, in 1900 there were 1.6 billion people on Earth. By 1950 this figure had grown to 2·7 billion. Demographers[2] estimate that by the end of the century, the Earth's population will be over 6·1 billion.

5 Demography is the study of the change in size, distribution[3] and character[4] of the human population; and the two most basic factors[5] in demography are the birth-rate and the death-rate. The former[6] expresses the number of children born per 1000 people per year. The latter[7] indicates the number of people who die per 1000 per year. If we consider the
10 Earth as a whole, we see that population growth or decline is caused by the difference between the number of births and deaths over a given period. There are normally more births than deaths, and this[8] is known as a natural increase in population.

For thousands of years, Man lived in a very primitive way. Before the
15 recent developments in agriculture, medicine and industry[9], life was difficult. It was hard to make a living from the soil without modern farming methods, and a few years of bad crops could mean famine[10] and therefore death – as it still does today in some parts of the world. Illnesses as mild and as common as influenza could kill a Stone-Age man[11]
20 weakened by hunger; appendicitis[12] (almost without risk today) was always fatal before the days of modern surgery[13]. Even childbirth was a hazardous process. Under these conditions, the human race needed to reproduce at a high rate just to keep in existence. But the size of the population did not change very rapidly, for without modern medicine,
25 many babies and young children died. So for a long time, the population grew very slowly. And this is still the case today in some parts of the world where the people live without the aids of modern technology[14].

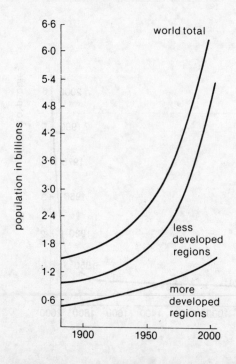

Fig. 1.1 World population growth in the 20th century

Study reading questions

1 1.6 → 2.7 → 6.1 billion in a century. In this context, what does *dramatically* mean?

2 Think of the word parts in *demo*cracy, bio*graph*y, and football*er*. Now work out what a *demographer* does.

3 Think of rivers and canals *distributing* water. What is meant by the *distribution* of the human population.

4 *Character* means a) moral strength, personality. b) different types. c) origins.

5 A *factor* is a *fact* which is used in a special way. From the example in this paragraph, what is the function of a factor?

6 *The former* links back to . . . ⁷ *The latter* links back to . . .

8 *What* is known as a natural increase in population?

9 What changes occurred during the Industrial Revolution, and when did it take place? (Use your dictionary.)

10 A few years of bad crops sometimes resulted in famine and death, therefore *famine* is . . .

11 What were the characteristics of this type of man?

12 What is cut out when you have *appendicitis*? Does your answer have another meaning? (Use your dictionary.)

13 A person who carries out surg . . . operations is called a surg . . . (Use your dictionary to complete this sentence, and include stress marks*.)

14 A tech . . . is a person who does tech . . . work. (Use your dictionary, and include stress marks*.)

Discussion questions

A Assume that the Earth's population is 5 billion. In a certain year, the birth-rate is 25 and the death-rate is 12 per 1000. Calculate the Earth's natural increase in population for that year.

B Can you think of situations in which there might be a natural *decrease* in population a) for a particular country, b) for the Earth as a whole?

C Using the items from the box below, copy and complete the following flowchart to show the structure of the second paragraph.

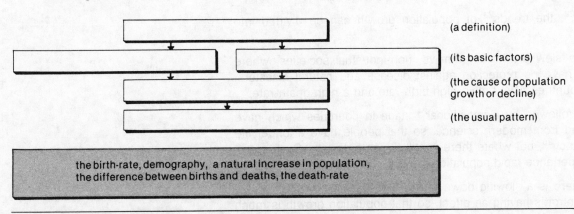

(a definition)

(its basic factors)

(the cause of population growth or decline)

(the usual pattern)

the birth-rate, demography, a natural increase in population, the difference between births and deaths, the death-rate

---

* For an explanation of *stress marks*, please refer to Appendix A, pp. 103 and 104.

It was only about two centuries ago – which is less than one-thousandth of man's existence – that the population growth pattern[15] changed (Fig.
30 1.2). New discoveries in medical science had a dramatic effect on the death-rate. Fewer children died in infancy, and adults lived longer. At the same time, the birth-rate stayed much the same – people were still having large families, even though they could expect most of their children to survive. Consequently[16], the population began to expand rapidly. And in
35 the 20th century, this acceleration in population growth has begun to cause severe social and economic problems in many developing countries.

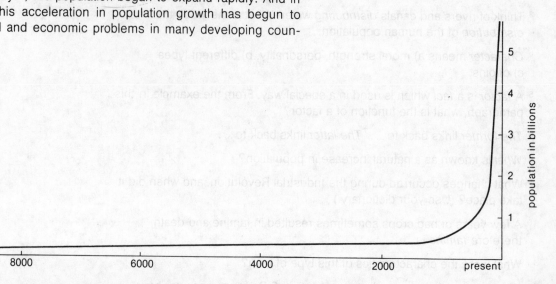

Fig. 1.2   The population explosion in modern times

Since man has discovered ways of treating illness and disease, and has thus reduced the death-rate, the only way to control population increase
40 is by lowering the birth-rate. In fact[17], as people in modern industrial societies began to move in order to work in the towns and factories, they found that a smaller family was easier to support[18]. So in Western Europe after the Industrial Revolution, the birth-rate did slow down as parents chose to have fewer children. More importantly, modern birth control
45 measures[19] have made it possible for parents to decide how many children to have.

But reducing the birth-rate is not as easy as that[20]. There are many religious, social and economic reasons why some parents do not want to control the number of children they have. For example, in some of the
50 less developed parts of the world, many children are needed to help work the land, or earn wages that supplement[21] the family income. To halt the population growth in such areas, it will first be necessary to raise the standard of living, so that parents do not need a large family.

To conclude[22], the trends[23] of population growth can be divided into
55 three stages:

1   There is slow growth in primitive, non-industrial societies, where people have no protection against disease and natural disasters. Such countries have both a high birth-rate and a high death-rate.

2   This is followed by a transitional[24] stage in countries which have
60   benefited from modern science, so that people have a longer life expectancy[25], but where there is still a high birth-rate. Such countries experience rapid population growth.

3   Then there is a slowing down of the birth-rate in countries where birth control is having an effect, so that population growth is much more gradual.

Study reading questions

¹⁵ *A population growth pattern* is:
a)   a pattern that shows the growth of population.
b)   a population that grows according to a pattern.
c)   a growth of the population pattern.
(Which way did you work to come to the correct answer? Left-to-right,
right-to-left, or centre outwards?)

¹⁶ What follows – a *summary* ⊤ of the preceding information, or the *result*
⟹ of it?

¹⁷ Which symbol best expresses the function of this 'signpost'?
a) (   )   b) ⇢→   c) ⟡⊷⚬

¹⁸ *Why* did they find it easier to support a smaller family?

¹⁹ *Birth control measures* are:
a)   the control of records of births.
b)   measurements of birth control.
c)   ways of controlling the number of births.
(Which way did you work to come to the correct answer? Left-to-right,
right-to-left, or centre outwards?)

²⁰ Reducing the birth-rate is not as easy as *what*?

²¹ Suppose there are two families – one with many children, all of whom are
working and earning money, and the other with only a few children.
Which family has the larger income? Therefore, when children
supplement the family income, they . . .

²² Which do we now expect?
a)   a *summary* ⊤ of the preceding information
b)   the *final part* ◯ of the passage
c)   the *result* ⟹ of the preceding information

²³ What *type* of information on population growth has the passage given
you? – a detailed historical account, specific examples, general
directions, theoretical arguments, etc.?

²⁴ The transitional stage comes between stages 1 and 3, therefore *transitional* means . . .

²⁵ *life expectancy* means:
a)   expecting a baby.
b)   expecting a certain standard of living.
c)   the number of years that the average person expects to live.

Discussion questions

D   Mention some of the discoveries in medical science that have had a
dramatic effect on the death-rate in recent times.

E   Does the passage give an example of a social, a religious or an economic
reason why some parents do not want to control the number of children
they have? Suggest examples of the other two types of reason.

F   Three stages of population growth are given. Can you suggest a *fourth* stage
that might develop in the future? What reasons can you offer for such a stage?

G   Find words or phrases that can be replaced by the following:
maintain
parents opted for smaller families
enabled
restrict their family size

Making Notes from a Talk

You will hear a short talk about the age structure of populations in different countries. As you listen, copy and complete the notes and diagrams. (Draw the diagrams in pencil to start with, in rough; you will be able to complete them more neatly later.)

Age structure

1 Mexico and Sweden

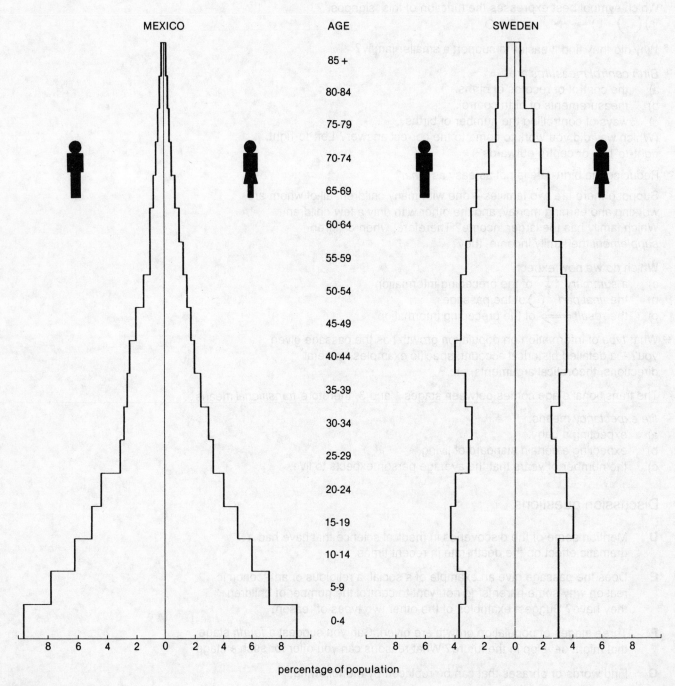

Mexico

Large . . . + low children's
. . . = . . .

Sweden

A constant . . . + a low . . .
in early and middle age = . . .

2   Effects of different age structures

2.1   Population growth

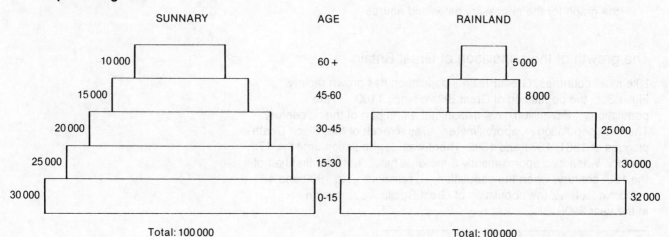

	SUNNARY	RAINLAND
women 15-45		
∴ children born (1:10)		
deaths 60 + (1:10)		
∴ population increase		

2.2   Working population

Mexico: the working population (aged . . . – . . .) = . . .% of the total population. Sweden: . . . (A country with a larger proportion of working people will . . .)

2.3   Education

Mexico has . . . the proportion of children aged . . ., ...

2.4   Employment

It is more difficult to find a job in a country with . . ., so . . .

Markers are devices that a speaker uses to divide up what he is saying. They help the listener to extract the main points from the talk, identify the introduction of a new topic, or follow successive stages in a line of reasoning. You heard the following markers in the *Age structure* talk. What was their significance?

1   '. . . I shall discuss two aspects of age structure . . .' (What are *aspects of X*?)

2   '. . . what do I mean by this term ''age structure''?' (Why did the speaker ask this question? What followed it?)

3   'So much for age structures themselves.' (What does *so much for X* tell you, i.e. what is the relationship between the information before and after this marker?)

4   'The point I am making, then, . . .' (What type of information does this marker introduce? Why did the speaker use this marker?)

Data Analysis and Comment

1 Study Fig. 1.3, then copy and complete the accompanying
description by adding the words and phrases from the box. Refer to
the graph for the necessary dates and figures.

The growth of the population of Great Britain

Like most countries, Great Britain's population has grown rapidly.
Fig. 1.3 . . . the population of Great Britain since 1100. . . . the
population . . . 2·5 million, . . . 4 million in the first part of the . . . century.
Then the population . . . approximately . . . as a result of the 'Black Death'
plagues of 1361, 1371 and 1382. There was . . . population until the 17th
century, when it . . . approximately 8 million. That . . . until the first half of
the 18th century, when the population . . ., reaching . . . in 1900 and 46
million in . . . If . . ., the population of Great Britain . . . . . . million
in the year 2000.

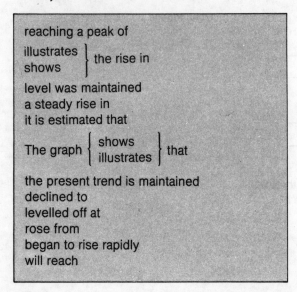

reaching a peak of

illustrates
shows   } the rise in

level was maintained
a steady rise in
it is estimated that

The graph { shows
            illustrates } that

the present trend is maintained
declined to
levelled off at
rose from
began to rise rapidly
will reach

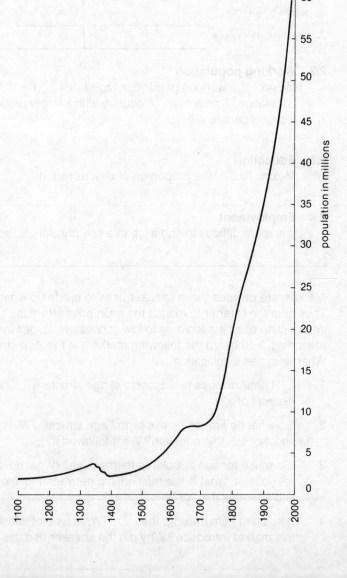

Fig. 1.3 The population of
Great Britain 1100–2000

2 Study Fig. 1.4, then copy and complete the accompanying description as four paragraphs. Draw six boxes to the left of your description as indicated. The graph itself, and the words and phrases in the box will help you to complete most of the gaps. You will need to use your own knowledge to complete the rest of the gaps, especially the final paragraph.

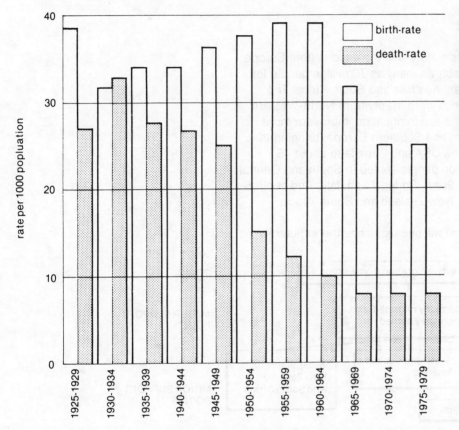

rose steadily
remained constant
plunged
dropping
rose sharply
declined rapidly
fell from

Fig. 1.4 Birth-rates and death-rates in Mauritius

Fig. 1.4 shows the changes in the . . .-rates and . . . in Mauritius from . . . to . . .

Except for the most recent decade, birth-rates have . . . .
The graph shows that the birth-rate . . . per 1000 in 1925–29 to . . . in 1930–34. It then . . ., reaching 39 per 1000 in . . ., before . . . to . . . per thousand in 1975–79.

Death-rates have . . . over the same period.
The only increase was from 1925–29 to 1930–34, when the death-rate . . . from . . . to . . . Since then, it has . . ., reaching . . . in 1975–79.

The death-rate has fallen over this period because . . .
On the other hand, the birth-rate . . .

The passage you have just completed has a planned structure. Indicate its structure by putting these phrases in the left-hand boxes:

DEATH-RATES IN GENERAL
BIRTH-RATE DETAILS
WHAT THE DATA SHOWS
BIRTH-RATES IN GENERAL
COMMENTS
DEATH-RATE DETAILS

Writing Paragraphs

The paragraph in **1**, and the paragraphs you will write in **2** and **3** form a complete text.

Modern migrations

1   Read the following paragraph:

> The biggest migration in man's history was the exodus from Europe during the 19th century. Probably as many as 70 million people left, to settle chiefly in the Americas, Australia and South Africa. The early emigrants to North America were mainly from North-Western Europe. But as communications and information improved, more people emigrated from Eastern and Southern Europe, bringing the total number of emigrants to the USA and Canada to about 45 million. Approximately 20 million people settled in South and Central America, coming chiefly from Spain, Portugal and Italy. And about 5 million emigrated to Australia, New Zealand and South Africa.

If you study the paragraph again, you will see that it has the structure:

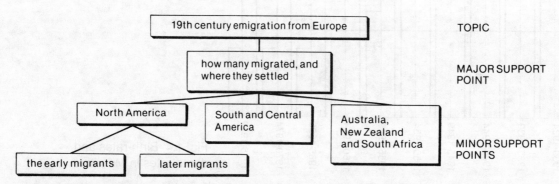

All paragraphs are *structured*, i.e. deliberately built around one topic. The topic is placed early in the paragraph (preferably the first sentence), so that the reader can more easily see what type of information the paragraph contains. The topic is developed by one or more major support points, all of which are connected with the topic. And major support points are often developed by minor support points.

2   Study the graph, then write a paragraph based on the structure:

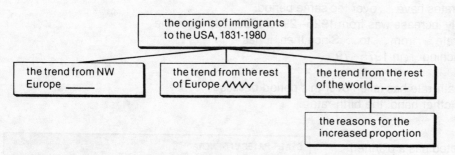

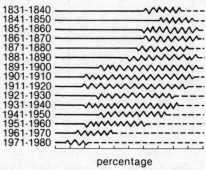

percentage

You may wish to use the following sentence beginnings:

During the period 1831–1980 . . . At the start of this period . . . Immigration from the rest of Europe, on the other hand, . . . And immigration from the rest of the world . . . The reasons for . . .

Fig. 1.5 Immigration to the USA 1831–1980

3 Answer the following questions to form a structured paragraph. You may wish to use the sentence beginnings in brackets after each question.

About a century ago, were there restrictions on migration? (Little more than a century ago, then, . . .) Are there restrictions now, and (if so) what form do they take? (But now . . . in the form of . . .) Would it be a good idea to return to unrestricted migration? (It might seem a good idea to . . .,) In general, what would the consequences be? (. . . but in practice . . .) What type of countries would people migrate to? (With easy transport, migrants would flood to countries which . . .) Then how would such countries change? (Such countries would quickly become . . .) What other problems would the host country face? (Moreover, it is very difficult . . . very large numbers . . . a different race, culture and way of life.) Therefore, what types of migrants are there nowadays? (As a result, . . .)

Draw a flowchart showing the structure of this paragraph, like the flowcharts for **1** and **2**. Indicate the topic, major support point(s), and minor support point(s).

Grammar Revision

In the following passage, ONE word has been omitted from each complete line. Marks (/) show where the words have been left out. Copy the passage, adding the words that you think have been omitted, e.g.

Population growth affects almost ^{1} <u>every</u> aspect of everyday life. This is ^{2} <u>because</u> a continual growth in the Earth's population forces us to change the ^{3} <u>way</u> we use the land.

(N.B. Number and underline the words that you add, as shown.)

Population growth and land use

Population growth affects almost/^{1} aspect of everyday life.
This is/^{2} a continual growth in the Earth's population
forces us to change the/^{3} we use the land. For example, an
expanding population needs more land/^{4} housing, shops and
industry. An expanding population also means that we need/^{5} grow
more food and build/^{6} hospitals, schools and roads. But the
area of land available/^{7} human use is fixed. In fact, only
about one-third of the Earth's surface is land, and/^{8} one-third
of that is suitable to live on. For example,/^{9} are large areas
of the Earth −/^{10} as deserts and the polar ice-caps − that
cannot at present support human life./^{11} course, there are low population
densities in some parts of the world,/^{12} in most cases the land
resources in such areas are already stretched/^{13} the limit. One
immediate answer to our population growth is to/^{14} deserts and
swamplands habitable. But the long-term answer/^{15} to stabilise
the Earth's population.

Unit two: Resources

Study Reading

Renewable and non-renewable resources

Natural resources are the materials that we need to run[1] our society. They come from the rocks, the oceans, and the tissues[2] of the animals and plants that live on the Earth with us. These materials are used directly[3], or processed and shaped into household products, clothes, machinery,
5 buildings, etc[4].

The thousands of different materials that we need to maintain our standard of living can be classified into renewable[6] and non-renewable[6] resources[5]. The former[7] include cotton, trees, rubber, animals and cellulose[8]. With proper management, such resources[9] will be available for
10 man's use indefinitely[10]. For example, as long as sufficient water, food and care are made available, animal populations such as sheep and cattle will continue to grow and reproduce.

Discussion questions

A Copy and complete the following table, giving at least one example of each from your own knowledge:

Natural resources that are found in –		
the rocks	the oceans	animals and plants
used directly		
processed and shaped		

B Do different societies attach the same value to a material? For example, what do you think a) were two of the most valuable materials to a Stone-Age man; b) were some of the most valuable 400 years ago; c) will be valuable in an industrialised society in the year 2050?

Study reading questions

1 In this context, *run* means
   a)   move very fast.
   b)   govern.
   c)   maintain.

2 Tissues are
   a)   a mass of cells.
   b)   very thin paper.
   c)   fossils.

3 Some materials are processed and shaped into household products, clothes, machinery, buildings, etc. Therefore, give examples of materials being used *directly*.

4 According to this sentence, are materials used in two ways, or three?

5 *What* can be classified into renewable and non-renewable resources? (Answer in one word.)

6 Define *renewable* and *non-renewable*, by analysing their word parts.

7 *What* include cotton, trees, rubber, animals and cellulose?

8 Use your dictionary to give a scientific definition of *cellulose*. How is it pronounced? (Write its transcription*, and include the stress mark.)

9 *Which* resources?

10 How long is this? (Use the context to tell you.)

Discussion questions

C   Using the items from the box below, copy and complete the flowchart to show the structure of these two paragraphs:

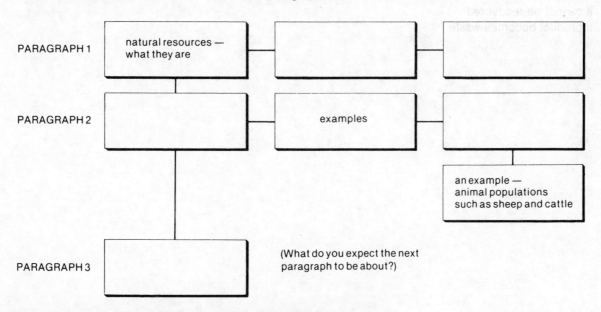

PARAGRAPH 1   natural resources — what they are

PARAGRAPH 2   examples

       an example — animal populations such as sheep and cattle

PARAGRAPH 3   (What do you expect the next paragraph to be about?)

Renewable resources; How they are used; The conditions for indefinite use; Where they come from

---

* For an explanation of the term *transcription*, please refer to Appendix A, p. 103.

Non[11]-renewable resources, on the other hand[12], occur on this planet in fixed quantities. The majority are minerals that are used by industry. Of 15 course[13], the mineral most in demand is iron ore, from which steel is refined. Fortunately[14], iron ore is plentiful, and stocks are expected to last at least 200 years. Other minerals – such as gold, copper, lead and zinc – are found in relatively small quantities.

Although non-renewable resources eventually return to the Earth after we 20 have used them, they do so[15] in different forms and are dispersed[16], and so it is often difficult to gather them to use again. Mercury is an example of an uncommon metal that is used in industrial processes, and in agriculture to kill fungi[17]. After use, it enters the atmosphere and oceans. Unfortunately[18], it is now so widely scattered that there is no way of get-25 ting it back. Once used, then, non-renewable resources frequently cannot be used again. When we have run out of[19] the easily-available supplies, there will be no more[20].

Yet[21] some materials do not *have*[22] to be returned to the environment once the useful life of a product is over. For instance, the materials that 30 constitute a car[23] remain in a concentrated form when the car's life is ended. And so the steel, copper, aluminium, etc. can be recovered, and reprocessed into new products. This is known as recycling.

Discussion questions

D Some materials are easier to recycle than others. Give examples of some that are easy to recycle, and some that are difficult. Can you explain why there is this difference?

E Find words or phrases that can be replaced by the following:
finite
most of them
abundant
it cannot be recovered
a product becomes waste

Study reading questions

11,22 Why are these italicised?

12 Complete the relationship indicated by this signpost:

 Non-renewable resources are
fixed in quantity.

13 Which symbol best expresses the function of this signpost word:
a) ( )
b) ∵
c) ⟹

14,18 Suggest suitable symbols for these signpost words.

15 They do *what*?

16 Which word later in the paragraph has approximately the same meaning?

17 Use your dictionary to give a scientific definition of *fungi*. How is it pronounced? (Write its transcription, and include the stress mark.)

19 Once used, non-renewable resources frequently cannot be used again, therefore *run out of* means...

20 No more *what*?

21 Which *two* of the following mean approximately the same as *yet* ▢ ?
however, consequently, furthermore, nonetheless

23 This means:
a)   the materials inside a car.
b)   the materials that a car is made of.
c)   the materials that make a car work.

Discussion questions

F   Copy and complete:

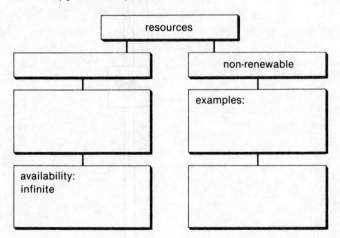

Making Notes from a Talk

You will hear a short talk about waste disposal. As you listen, copy and complete the notes and diagrams. (Draw the diagrams in pencil to start with, in rough; you will be able to complete them more neatly later.)

Waste disposal

1   Why are new methods of dealing with waste necessary?
1.1 ...
1.2 ...

2   Where does it come from?

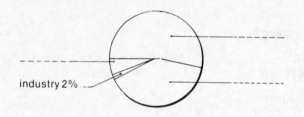

industry 2%

3   Where does it go to?

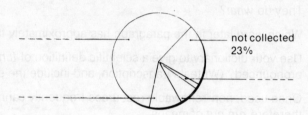

not collected 23%

4   Present methods of domestic waste disposal

	ADVANTAGES	DISADVANTAGES
open dumps		
landfill		
incineration		

5   Waste disposal in an apartment block

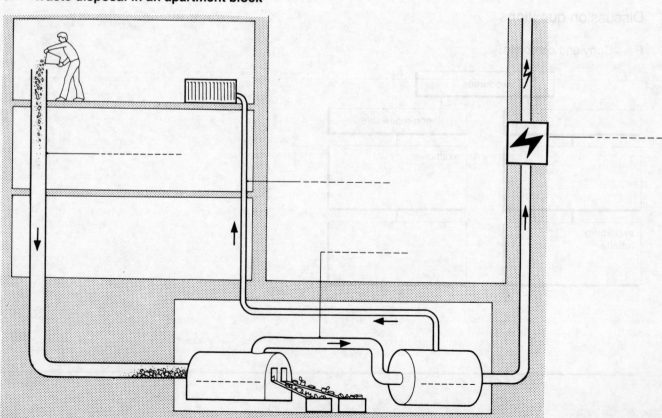

6 Materials recovery centres of the future

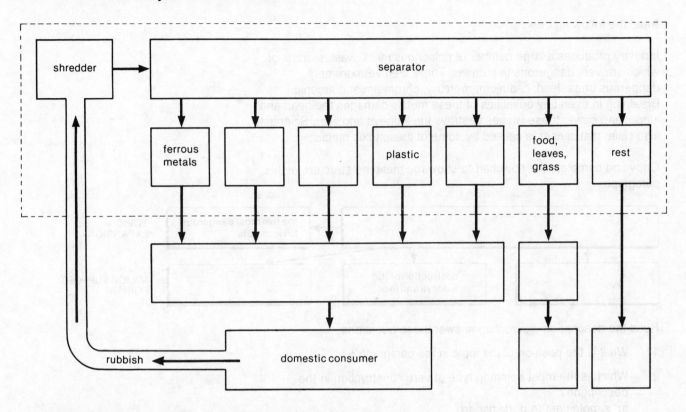

You heard the following *markers* in the *waste disposal* talk. What was their significance?

1 'Let's firstly talk about where our waste comes from. Basically, there are four sources of waste...' (The speaker is saying something in two different ways, in order to make his meaning clearer. What is it? Also, what is meant by *basically*?)

2 'What about landfill?' (Why did the speaker ask this question? What followed it?)

3 'This business of putting household waste in a bin outside the house, and having the bin emptied each week into a lorry – it's very unscientific for the 20th century, isn't it!' (What is the key word in this marker, that lets you know what type of information is to follow? What type of information *does* come next?)

You also heard a number of *colloquial expressions* (expressions commonly used in informal conversation), which the lecturer often uses to make his lecture more interesting. What did the following colloquial expressions mean?

4 'Yet things *are* beginning to change. We're slowly getting the message that we can't go on indefinitely throwing our waste away...' (What happens when you *get the message*?)

5 '...20th century societies now produce so much waste that it simply doesn't make sense to deal with it in this way.' (Explain *it doesn't make sense*.)

6 'Domestic rubbish is usually disposed of in one of three ways, all of which have their pros and cons.' (What are *pros and cons*?)

7 'On the credit side, incineration can handle about 80% of domestic rubbish... But on the debit side, it's expensive...' (Explain the terms *debit* and *credit*. In which profession are they normally used, and what do they mean in that profession?)

Writing Descriptions

Read the following description:

Industry produces a large number of poisonous metal wastes, most of which are very dangerous to humans. There are five extremely dangerous ones: lead, cadmium, mercury, chromium and arsenic. Breathing in even tiny quantities of these metals damages the heart and lungs; and eating these wastes destroys the kidneys and liver. Scientists also claim that cancer is caused by some of these toxic metals.

Copy and complete the flowchart to show the meaning structure of this paragraph:

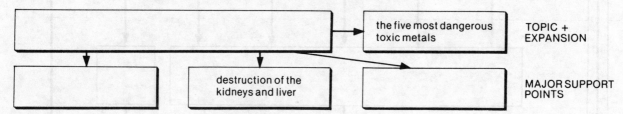

Read the description again, then answer these questions:

1   What is the position of the topic in the paragraph?

2   Which is the most common type of verb construction in the description?
   a) simple past (e.g. *damaged*)
   b) simple present (e.g. *damages* or *damage*)
   c) passive (e.g. *was* or *were damaged*)

3   Which other type of verb construction is used in this description?

4   What do you notice about sentence length and complexity?

Your answers to these questions indicate the major features of written descriptions. Using these features, and remembering the importance of paragraph structure, write descriptions of:

a) A materials recovery centre. (Refer to the diagram on p. 23).

b) The structure and temperature distribution
    of the Earth's atmosphere.

c) An underground waste disposal well.

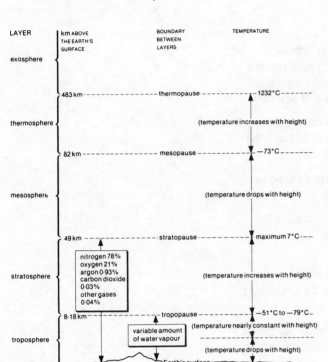

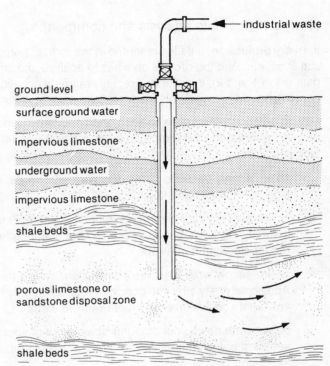

Grammar Revision

In the following passage, ONE word has been omitted from each line.
Marks (/) show where the words have been left out. Copy the passage,
adding the words that you think have been omitted, e.g.

Water is a renewable resource, and is abundant. However, most [1] of it
is not in a form suitable for use [2] by man. Even the very large
amounts [3] that are available are distributed unequally over the globe.

(N.B. Number and underline the words that you add, as shown.)

The world's water supply

Water is a renewable resource, and is abundant. However, most[1]/ it
is not in a form suitable for use[2]/ man. Even the very large
amounts[3]/ are available are distributed unequally over the globe.
The real question we need to ask is[4]/ there is or
will[5]/ a shortage of usable water. About 97·2% of all the world's
water is[6]/ the salty oceans. Of the remaining 2·8%,
all[7]/ about 0·32% is tied up in ice-caps and glaciers,
lies too deep under the Earth[8]/ recover, or is in
the atmosphere or topsoil. And[9]/ the fresh ground water and
surface[10]/ (lakes and rivers) remaining, over 99%
is either[11]/ expensive to get, is not readily available, or is
polluted. So the total[12]/ of usable water is about 0.003% of the total
supply on Earth – or about 9 drops[13]/ 50 litres. Even so,
we seem to have[14]/ ample supply but for three factors:
very unequal distribution, rapidly rising demand,[15]/ increasing
pollution of water supplies[16]/ urban centres.

Data Analysis and Comment

How to tackle data analysis and comment

In every profession, data is presented in the form of graphs, tables, statistics, etc. And the professional has to *analyse and comment on* that data (as in **1** and **2**), in order to direct his reader's attention to significant content, and to persuade his reader to take a certain course of action.

Having practised some data analysis and comment in Unit one, it is perhaps now worthwhile looking at ways in which this skill might best be tackled:

DO NOT simply translate all the data back into words. Instead, select significant trends and items.

DO NOT present your comments in one long continuous answer. Instead, 'signpost' your reader with short paragraphs, in a reader-oriented framework.

DO NOT simply write what you see as significant in the data. Additionally, say why you consider your comments to be significant, and what conclusions can be drawn from them.

DO NOT write down your thoughts straight out of your head. Instead, set them out in an organised format, for the reader's benefit.

DO NOT forget to state the obvious.

1 Study Fig. 2.1, then copy and complete the accompanying description by adding the words and phrases from the box. Refer to the graph for the necessary percentages, and complete the final sentence from your own knowledge.

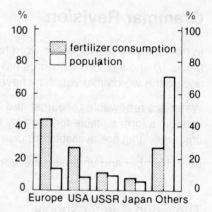

Fig. 2.1 Fertilizer consumption
in relation to population

Fig. 2.1 ... fertilizer ... population. It is clear that developed countries ... a ... of the world's fertilizer. For example, the USA, with ... % of the population, ... % of the fertilizer. And Europe, with ... % of the population, consumes ... %. Japan, however, consumes an almost ... of the world's fertilizer (... %) ... its population (... %). But the ... of fertilizer used by other countries (mostly developing) is small ... population. The reason for this is ...

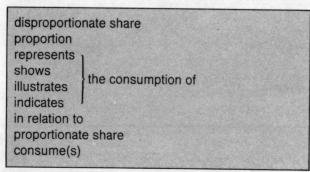

disproportionate share
proportion
represents ⎫
shows   ⎬ the consumption of
illustrates   ⎪
indicates   ⎭
in relation to
proportionate share
consume(s)

2 Study Fig. 2.2, then copy and complete the accompanying description as four paragraphs. Draw seven boxes beside your description as indicated. The graph itself, and the words and phrases in the box in **1** will help you complete most of the gaps. You will need to use your own knowledge to complete the rest.

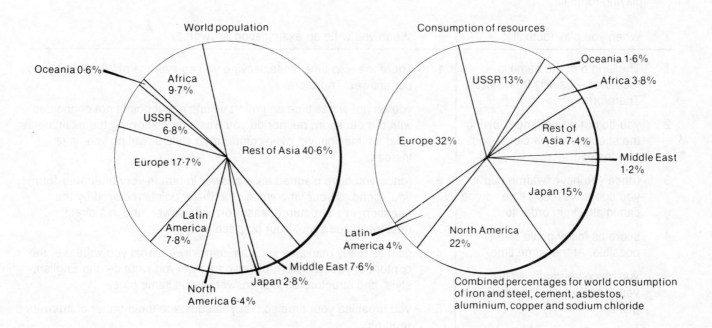

Fig. 2.2 The consumption of resources in relation to population

Fig. 2.2 . . . in different parts of the world . . . .

It is clear that the major industrial regions . . . .
In fact, Japan, . . . , . . . and . . . together consume 82%,
yet . . . of the world's population. Of these countries,
Japan (with . . . of the population) consumes . . . . North
America . . . . And Europe . . .

Developing countries, on the other hand, ...
In particular, . . . consumes 7·4% but has . . . . And
Africa . . .

. . . the world is using its resources unfairly. As a result,
. . . between developed and developing countries.
In order to . . . these differences, developed countries
should . . .

3 Indicate the structure of the description you have just completed, by putting the following items in the boxes:

RECOMMENDATIONS
DEVELOPING REGIONS' CONSUMPTION: POPULATION
CONCLUSION
INDUSTRIAL REGIONS' CONSUMPTION: POPULATION
EXAMPLES OF DEVELOPING REGIONS
WHAT THE DATA SHOWS
EXAMPLES OF INDUSTRIAL REGIONS

Writing Examination Answers

1 General advice

Writing an examination answer in continuous English is similar to playing football.

When you play football . . .	When you write an examination answer . . .
1 The length of the game is restricted – usually 90 minutes. Therefore,	1 There are also time limits, leaving you an average of 20–30 minutes per answer. Therefore,
2 you do not waste time showing the spectators how clever you are. Instead,	2 you do not waste time and effort writing about points not connected with the question; neither do you waste time showing the examiner what an imaginative, over-complicated style of writing you have. Instead,
3 (once you have 'warmed up'), you spend as much time as you can in attack, in order to	3 (once you have planned each answer in turn in very brief note-form) you spend all your time writing the major points required by the question, in a structured, easy-to-read answer, and in a direct, uncomplicated style. Your purpose is to
4 score as many goals as possible. At the same time,	4 gain as many marks as you can, primarily for *what* you write (i.e. the content of your answer); but also for *how* you write it – the English, style, and structure of your answer. At the same time,
5 you 'pace yourself', so that your energy lasts the whole game.	5 you organise your time so that you complete the number of answers required.

2 Instructions

Examination questions frequently include an instruction, e.g. *describe, discuss, write notes on, define, compare, outline*, etc. It is important to understand what the examiner means by these instructions, so that you can plan your answer accordingly.

3 The instruction *describe*

A dictionary definition of *describe*: 'to state the major characteristics of something'

Describe questions require you to state the appearance of something (X), or to state the major characteristics or aspects of X. Note the word *state*, i.e. you are *not* asked to comment on X, or to give your personal opinion about it. A possible approach to describe questions is:

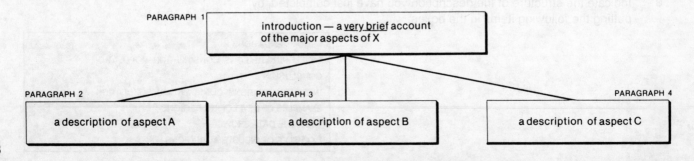

Note also that the structure of this examination answer limits itself to the major (most important) aspects of X. You will not have time to write about minor aspects, or to go into detail. The purpose of the *very brief* introduction (1 or 2 sentences) is to 'get the examiner on your side' by making it plain what you are going to write about, and how you are going to structure your answer. Notice also that the suggested structure does not contain a conclusion – a conclusion is only occasionally necessary (e.g. in a *discuss* question, pp. 40 and 41).

When writing *describe* answers, you should of course remember the features of written descriptions that you noted in the paragraph on p. 24.

Study and discuss the following diagram:

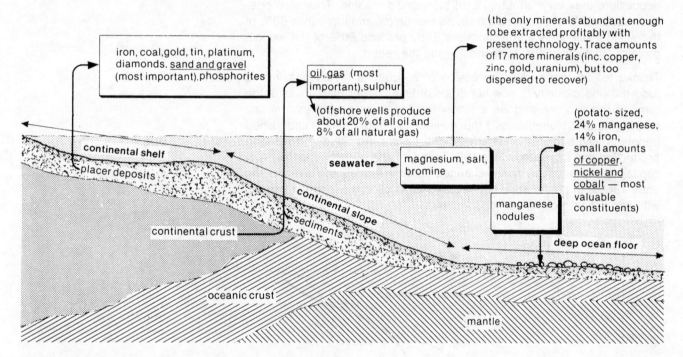

Write an answer to the following examination question:

Describe the different types of mineral resources found in the ocean.

A possible answer structure is:

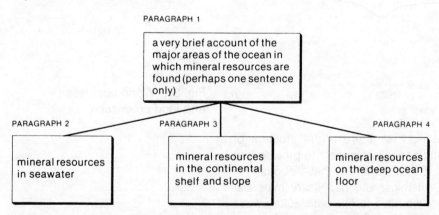

Seawater, the continental shelf and slope, and *the deep ocean floor* are paragraph topics, so mention them as soon as possible in their respective paragraphs, so that the examiner can immediately see what the subject matter of each paragraph is. Underline these paragraph topics in your answer.

Unit three: Food

Study Reading

Population growth and food supply

About two-thirds of the world's population live in what are loosely called 'developing countries'. Of course, strictly speaking[1] *all* countries are developing, but the term[2] is used to describe those which are undeniably[3] poor. Although the rich countries have only about 34% of the world's
5 population, they earn about 90% of the world's income. They also possess about 90% of the world's financial resources, and more than 80% of the world's scientists and technicians. They produce 80% of the world's protein – including 70% of its meat – and they eat it.

Thanks to[4] an impressive succession of agricultural revolutions, man's
10 food-growing capacity is now hundreds of times larger than it was at the turn[5] of the century, and we are now feeding more people than at any time in history. Nonetheless[6], the number of hungry and malnourished people is also larger[7] than at any time in history. Admittedly[8], total food production has increased since 1961 in most parts of the world. Yet[8] per
15 capita[9] food production is little changed from the inadequate levels of the early 1960s. In short, world and regional production have barely kept up with population growth, as Fig. 3.1 shows.

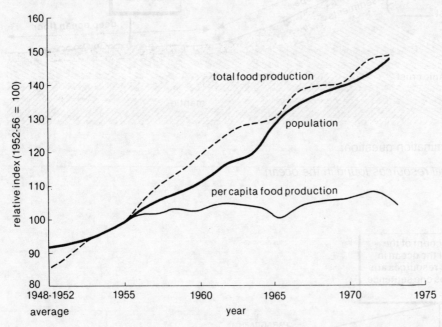

Fig. 3.1 World population and food production

There appear to be five food problems. First, there is the problem of quantity – of every human being getting enough calories[10] to provide him
20 with the energy to work and progress. Second, there is that[11] of quality – of everyone getting enough protein, vitamins, and necessary minerals. Next there is the matter of distribution: we have to find satisfactory ways of transporting, storing and issuing food. Then there is the problem of poverty: many people in developing countries do not have money to buy
25 food in sufficient quantity and of sufficient quality. And last, we must find ways of avoiding ecological[12] side-effects[13]. In other words, we must be able to grow enough food without further degrading[14] our land, water and
30 air.

Study reading questions

1 Some teachers are *strict*. Therefore, what does the phrase *strictly speaking* mean? Which word in this paragraph means the opposite of *strictly*?

2 *Which* term?

3 The root of this word is *deny*. Analyse the other word parts to work out the meaning of *undeniably*.

4 *Thanks to* is a special way of saying *because of*. What is the difference?

5 What do you do when you *turn the page of a book*? Therefore, *at the turn of the century* means . . .

6 Which *two* of these signpost words mean approximately the same as nonetheless :*however, on the contrary, yet, that is to say*

7 *What* is also larger? (Answer in one word.)

8 Consider also:
   Admittedly, oil is expensive. *Yet* the world depends on it.
   What is the relationship between the *admittedly* and *yet* pieces of information in these two sentences? Which is the more important?

9 Which part of the body usually receives *capital punishment*? What do you think *per capita* means?

10 Use the context to help you to define *calories*.

11 *What*?

12 Use your dictionary to define *ecology*. (Include the stress mark.)

13 Examine the two words that make up *side-effects*, in order to work out its meaning.

14 Consider *de*crease, *de*scend; and under*grad*uate, *grad*uate, post*grad*uate. What does *degrading* mean?

Discussion questions

A   Draw a graph to represent the data given in the first paragraph, in order to bring out forcibly the point being made.

B   Mention some of the agricultural revolutions referred to at the start of the second paragraph.

C   Discuss the causes and consequences of the trends shown in Fig. 3.1.

D   Find words or phrases that can be replaced by the following:
poorly-fed
ever before
virtually the same as
hardly

E   The five-stage train of thought in the second paragraph can be expressed as a series of boxes. Which series best expresses the writer's thoughts? (Justify your answer.)

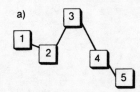
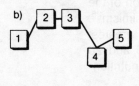
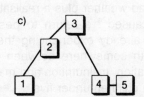

A number of proposals have been made to improve food quantity and
30 quality. An obvious and very necessary one[15] is to limit population
growth. Another[15] is to increase the amount of land under cultivation by
clearing forests and by irrigating arid[16] land. Furthermore[17], the ocean
(comprising 70% of the Earth's surface) is a potential source of more
food, and there have been developments recently in the use of noncon-
35 ventional proteins and synthetic[18] foods. And last, various attempts are
being made to increase the yield per hectare by developing or selecting
new genetic hybrids[19] of plants (the 'Green Revolution'), by increasing
the use of fertilizers[20], water, pesticides[20], and herbicides[20], and by using
modern agricultural and management techniques in poorer countries.

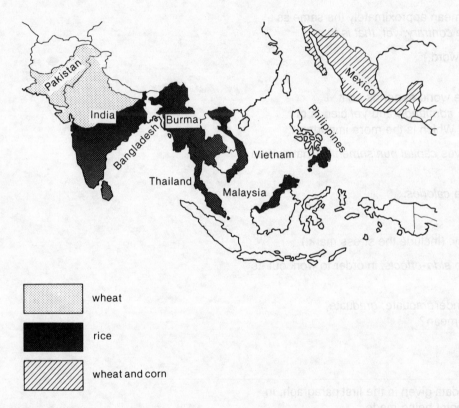

wheat

rice

wheat and corn

Fig. 3.2 Green Revolution
countries

40 But the basic facts remain, which are that the world's population is increasing at a rate of about 3% p.a. If food production can also be increased by 3% p.a., this will provide for human needs only at the present
inadequate level. Something better is needed. Yet[21] many countries are
already failing to increase their rate of food production by 3% annually.
45 The situation is particularly disturbing because population increase and
inadequate food production are both worse in the very[22] countries that
are already short of food.

Are we, then, doomed to massive famines in coming decades? There is
no easy answer to this controversial question. The introduction of new
50 high-yield wheat and rice in parts of Asia and Africa since 1967 created[23]
a wave of optimism[25]. But by 1973, bad weather plus a realisation of the
limitations of this increase in yield caused[24] a return to pessimism[25].
Some experts point out that we are already experiencing the greatest
famine in the history of mankind, with somewhere between 5 and 20
55 million human beings dying from starvation, malnutrition and malnutrition-
32 caused diseases[26] each year. Half are children under five.

Study reading questions

15 A very necessary *what*? Another *what*?

16 The proposal is to improve food quantity and quality by *irrigating arid* land. If you know the meaning of either *irrigating* or *arid*, use the context to work out the meaning of the other word. (If you do not know the meaning of either word, look up *one* in the dictionary.)

17 Which symbol best expresses the inter-sentence relationship expressed by *furthermore*:
   a) ⟹
   b) +
   c) ( )

18 Nylon and plastic are examples of *synthetic materials*. What type of foods are *synthetic foods*?

19 Use your dictionary to give a scientific definition of *hybrid*. Then use the definition, and the first four letters of *genetic*, to explain the meaning of the phrase *genetic hybrids*.

20 Distinguish between *fertilizers, pesticides* and *herbicides*. (Use your dictionary, if necessary.)

21 Choose *one* word from each of the sentences before and after *yet*, to complete the relationship it indicates:

22 Suppose you want to borrow a particular book from the library on the subject of food. The library owns 100 books on food, and there are 99 on the shelves. *The very book* you want has already been borrowed by someone else. What does *very* mean in this context?

23 *What* created a wave of optimism? (Give the extended subject, and its principal noun).

24 *What* caused a return to pessimism? (Give the extended subject, and its principal noun(s).)

25 Which words help you to understand the meanings of *optimism* and *pessimism*?

26 *Malnutrition-caused diseases* means:
   a) malnutrition that is caused by diseases.
   b) diseases that are caused by malnutrition.

   (Which way did you work to come to the correct answer? Right-to-left, or left-to-right?)

Discussion questions

F What is the 'Green Revolution', and why is it so called?

G Summarise the information in the fourth paragraph of this passage (top of p. 32) by copying and completing the table:

PROPOSALS TO IMPROVE FOOD QUANTITY AND QUALITY	
WHAT	HOW
1 limit population growth	
2	
3	
4	
5	

H In the final paragraph, the writer says: 'There is no easy answer to this controversial question'. From the evidence of this paragraph, does he offer an answer? What is *your* answer?

Making Notes from a Talk

A useful way of speeding up your note-making is to use *abbreviations* of words that are commonly used. The following are common standard abbreviations:

ABBREVIATION	MEANING
approx.	approximately, about
cf.	compared with, compare
esp.	especially
etc.	etcetera, and so on
excl.	excluding
i.e.	in other words, that is to say
incl.	including
max.	maximum
min.	minimum
N.B.	take special note of
p.a.	each year
viz.	namely
w.e.f.	with effect from

From now on, use abbreviations in your note-making wherever possible.

You will hear a short talk about a particular aspect of food. As you listen, copy and complete the notes and diagrams. (Draw the diagrams in pencil to start with, in rough; you will be able to complete them more neatly later.) Give your notes a suitable heading and sub-headings when you have finished.

_____ (heading)

1   World fish catch
Fish provides....

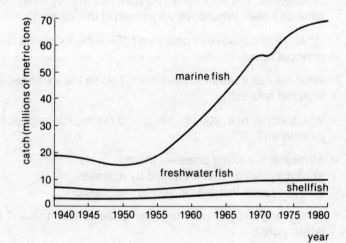

2 _____ (sub-heading)

Developed countries...,
e.g. Norway...; cf.
India..., Nigeria...,
Colombia...

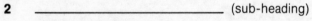

**3   Reasons for low fish consumption in
developing countries**
3.1 ...   e.g. Peru ...
3.2 ...
3.3 ...

4   _____ (sub-heading)
4.1 Danger: ...
4.2 In the year 2000 ...
4.3 But ...

5   Aquaculture and mariculture (hope for the future)
5.1 Aquaculture = ..., e.g. Japan ...
5.2 Mariculture = ...

_____

You heard the following *markers* in the talk. What was their significance?

1   'So, people in developing countries eat comparatively little fish,
     although it's abundant. I find this rather puzzling, don't you?' (Since
     the speaker finds this fact *puzzling*, what type of information do you
     expect him to give you next?)

2   'Well, one reason is that ...' (Will there be *another* reason? How do
     you know?)

3   'I started off this lecture by saying that one means of increasing food
     production is to increase the amount of fish that we catch.' (Which
     are the key words in this marker that indicate the type of information
     to come?)

4   'But you mustn't get too depressed by all this!' (Think of *how* the
     speaker said this – do you expect good news or bad news?)

You heard the following *colloquial expressions*. What did they mean?

5   'So it stands to reason that one means of increasing food production
     is to increase the amount of fish that we catch.' (What is the
     meaning of *it stands to reason*?)

6   '*Can* we continue to extract more and more fish from the ocean? Of
     course, we must be careful not to kill the goose that lays the golden
     egg!' (Do you know the story of the goose and the golden egg?
     What does it mean in this context?)

7   '... 120 million tons of fish by the year 2000 would still give us a per
     capita fish consumption *lower* than today's level. Do you get my
     point?' (What do you do when you *get someone's point*?)

Lectures also contain vocabulary that is common to a wide range of
subjects, but which you are unlikely to hear in everyday speech. We shall
call this *formal vocabulary*. You heard examples of formal vocabulary in
the talk. What did the following mean?

8   'Consumption of fish in Norway, for instance, is about 60 kg *per
     capita* per annum.'

9   '... fish exports amount to more than 25% of the country's annual
     revenue.'

10   '... the *maximum yield* by the year 2000 will be about 120 million
     tons.'

11   '... with a *projected* population growth of 3% per annum, ...'

Data Analysis and Comment

1 Study Fig. 3.3, then answer the questions below it to form an accompanying paragraph. The answer fragments in brackets will help you.

The availability of cropland

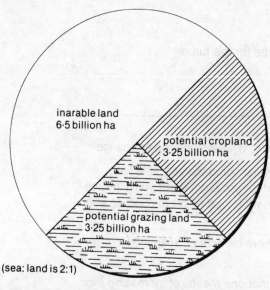

inarable land
6·5 billion ha

potential cropland
3·25 billion ha

potential grazing land
3·25 billion ha

(sea: land is 2:1)

Fig. 3.3 Land usage

What is the total area of the Earth? (The total area . . .) What percentage of this is sea? (But . . .) What area is land? (Therefore, . . .) What percentage of land is inarable? (However, as Fig. 3.3 illustrates, in practice . . .) Why is this? (, because . . .) What area is only suitable for grazing? (Of the remaining 6·5 billion ha, . . .) Therefore, how much is potentially available for cultivating crops? (, leaving . . .)

2 Study Fig. 3.4, then answer the questions below to form an accompanying three-paragraph text. The answer fragments in brackets will help you.

Limits on cultivating potential cropland

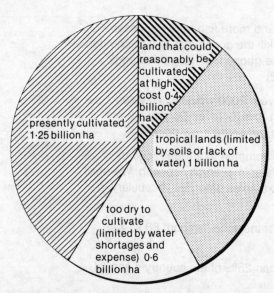

land that could reasonably be cultivated at high cost 0·4 billion ha

presently cultivated 1·25 billion ha

tropical lands (limited by soils or lack of water) 1 billion ha

too dry to cultivate (limited by water shortages and expense) 0·6 billion ha

Fig. 3.4 Reasons for the limits to the amount of land that can be cultivated

(This Fig. is a more detailed version of the 'potential cropland 3·25 billion ha' section of Fig. 3.3, above.)

What is the total area of potential cropland on Earth? (There are . . .) What area is presently cultivated? (However, as Fig. 3.4 shows, only . . .) By how much does it appear we might increase the area of land under cultivation? (It would appear, therefore, . . .) Is this in fact possible? (Unfortunately, . . .)

How much of the uncultivated land is in the tropics? (For example, approximately . . . % . . .) What type of climate is there in these regions? (These regions . . . abundant rainfall . . . long or continuous growing seasons.) What is the soil like? (But . . . poor) Why is this? (, because . . . high temperatures . . . dead organic material decays rapidly.) What happens to the nutrients released in this manner? (. . . taken up rapidly by the vegetation . . . most of the nutrients are contained in the vegetation, not . . .) What happens when the lush vegetation is stripped away? (. . . heavy rainfall . . . remaining nutrients out of the soil.) Is there sometimes a further problem? (A further . . . a high content of iron and aluminium.) Therefore, what happens to the soil after the vegetation is cleared? (. . . the hot tropical sun bakes . . . called laterites . . . growing food.)

Where are most of the remaining potentially arable soils found? (. . . dry areas.) What is the limiting factor in such areas? (. . . water.) How can these soils be made productive? (. . . irrigation . . . enormously large and expensive water transport projects.) What progress has been made in opening up new agricultural lands through irrigation? (However, considerable progress . . . In fact . . . 1800 – 8 million ha; 1900 – 40; today – 160; 2000 – (?) 280)

Grammar Revision

In the following passage, ONE word has been omitted from each complete line. Marks (/) show where the words have been left out. Copy the passage, adding the words that you think have been omitted, e.g.

In [1] the Green Revolution, scientists collected thousands of
genetic varieties of rice and wheat from [2] all over the world, . . .

(N.B. Number and underline the words that you add, as shown.)

The Green Revolution

In / Green Revolution, scientists collected thousands of
genetic varieties of rice and wheat from / over the world,
and cross-bred them / they found varieties that produced
high yields and were more resistant / disease. But these
hybrid strains / from four to seven times as much water
per hectare, and / is a limiting factor in some areas.
Moreover, / achieve high yields, the new varieties need
much / fertilizer per hectare than the previous varieties
did. Unfortunately, many developing countries / been
experiencing fertilizer shortages / the price of oil began
to / in the early 1970s. Scientists are also aware of the danger
of relying on only a / strains of rice and wheat. They
remember the Irish potato famine / 1845 and 1850, when
potato blight wiped / the single crop that fed almost all
the population. One million people died. Scientists / therefore
collecting and maintaining varieties of food crops from / over
the world.

Cohesion in Writing

Study the following paragraph:

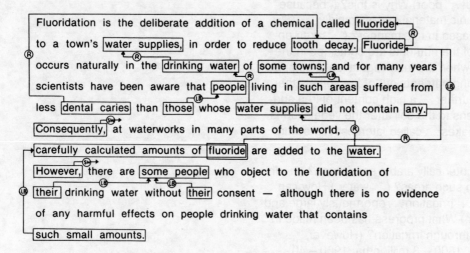

A good writer makes the words and phrases within a text *cohere* (stick together), so that the text can be read more smoothly and with greater comprehension. The three most important ways of improving cohesion in your writing are to use:

1 Signpost words (SW) (pp. 4–6)
2 Linking-back devices (LB) (p. 3)
3 Repetition (R)

There are two types of repetition – *exact* and *parallel*. Give examples of each from the paragraph above.

In your own writing, remember the importance of cohesion.

Now copy (double-spacing) the first paragraph of the reading passage on p. 30, and mark the various types of cohesion as in the paragraph above.

Writing Definitions

Read the following definition:

A food additive is a chemical which is deliberately added to food for a specific purpose. The purpose might be to retard spoilage, to enhance flavour, to add colour, to increase nutrition, or to improve texture. For example, colour dyes are added to soft drinks, butter and sausages to increase sales appeal. Vitamins and essential amino acids are added to bread and flour to replace nutrients lost in processing. And saccharin is added to sweets and ice-cream to enhance their taste.

Complete the flowchart to show the meaning structure of this definition paragraph:

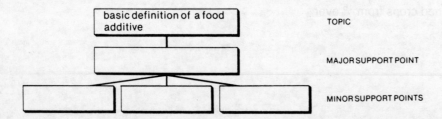

The usual structure of a definition is a single-sentence basic definition, followed by an expansion of one or more points. (Which point(s) in the basic definition of a food additive were expanded in the rest of the definition?) The structure of a definition, then, is:

A BASIC DEFINITION OF X + ONE OR MORE OF . . .	A DESCRIPTION OF THE ORIGIN OF X AN EXPLANATION OF WHAT X IS USED FOR A BREAKDOWN OF X INTO ITS MAIN PARTS ONE OR MORE EXAMPLES A DESCRIPTION OF ITS MAJOR PROPERTIES A DESCRIPTION OF ITS OVERALL APPEARANCE

Which type of expansion you choose will depend on the purpose for which you are writing the definition.

The basic definition itself usually has a specific structure, which is:

THING TO BE DEFINED (X) + DEFINING VERB	'FAMILY' TO WHICH X BELONGS	CHARACTERISTICS THAT DISTINGUISH X FROM OTHER MEMBERS OF ITS 'FAMILY'
A food additive is A food additive may be defined as	a chemical	which is deliberately added to food for a specific purpose.

Complete the following basic definitions:

THING TO BE DEFINED (X) + DEFINING VERB	'FAMILY' TO WHICH X BELONGS	CHARACTERISTICS THAT DISTINGUISH X FROM OTHER MEMBERS OF ITS 'FAMILY'
Rice is		
		made of glass, with a narrow neck, for storing liquids.
A whale may be defined as		
		which comes from the flesh of an ox, bull or cow.
	an insecticide	

Write full definitions (i.e. basic definition + expansion) of the following:
1 a whale   2 malnutrition   3 the Green Revolution

Writing Examination Answers

1   The components of a question

To score high marks in an examination, you must fully understand what a question means. And to understand the question, you must search for certain components. All examination questions contain a few words that form the *subject matter* of the question. Most questions also contain an *aspect* of that subject matter, and an *instruction*. Sometimes there is a *restriction or expansion* of the subject matter, e.g.

INSTRUCTION	ASPECT	SUBJECT MATTER	RESTRICTION OR EXPANSION OF SUBJECT MATTER
Describe	the industrial uses of	the mineral resources	on the deep ocean floor.

The subject matter is the most important component of a question. You should find the subject matter first, then its restriction or expansion. Next, search for the aspect of the subject matter. This is the *angle* or *point of view* on the subject matter. Often, the aspect is a phrase ending in *of*, e.g. *the importance of, the contribution of*. Finally, identify the instruction (which usually comes at the beginning of the question), and decide what it means.

Tabulate the components of the following questions in the same way. If a question does not contain one of the four components, put a dash (–).

1 Discuss the social and economic consequences of a high birth-rate.
2 Explain the increase in the production of synthetic foods in the last 20 years.
3 What is the contribution of the United Nations' FAO (Food and Agriculture Organisation) in increasing food production?
4 Write notes on the feasibility of recycling non-renewable materials, particularly those contained in industrial waste.

In the same way, tabulate the components of recent examination questions in one of your main subjects.

2   The instruction *discuss*

A dictionary definition of *discuss*: 'to examine by argument, to debate'

Discuss questions usually present a debatable statement (sometimes in the form of a quotation) about a certain topic. The candidate is expected to examine the *statement as a whole*, i.e. not just one word or one part of the statement, and not the topic itself.

Consider the examination question:

Discuss the Mindonian government's attempts to improve the diet of schoolchildren by distributing powdered milk.

(What is the *subject matter*? Does the subject have a *restriction* or *expansion*, and an *aspect*?)

Which set of paragraph topics best answers the question? What do you consider is wrong with the other two answers?

ANSWER 1 – differences between natural and powdered milk
          – nutritional content of powdered milk
          – advantages of powdered milk (transport, storage, distribution, cost, etc.)
          – use of powdered milk in children's diets in different countries
          – manufacture of powdered milk

ANSWER 2 – constituents of a balanced diet
          – major dietary problems in developing countries
          – reasons for those problems
          – attempts made by developing countries to improve the diet of their citizens
          – difficulties encountered (fertilizer, cost, education)

ANSWER 3 – diet of Mindonian schoolchildren before the introduction of powdered milk
          – extent to which powdered milk improved the diet
          – average height, weight and health of Mindonian schoolchildren before and after the introduction of powdered milk
          – dietary deficiencies that still remain
          – problems of supply and distribution

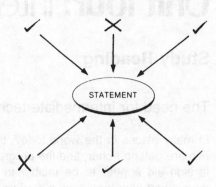

As you saw in the answer that you chose, in a *discuss* question you should examine the whole statement from a number of angles, some of which may support (✓) the statement, while others are critical (x) of it, i.e.

The examiners are not looking for a fixed list of points to be marked right or wrong. Instead, they are looking for informed, relevant observations, supported by sound reasoning and by evidence of thought and reading on the subject matter. At the end of your answer, you should tie your major points together in a conclusion paragraph. Your conclusion will probably be a 'subtraction sum', in which you compare your points supporting and criticising the statement, and arrive at an overall opinion. In a *discuss* answer (as in many others) you will gain more marks by examining the statement from four or five viewpoints than from only one or two.

Consider the following question:

What is DDT? Discuss the contribution of DDT to human progress. (Identify the *subject matter*, the *aspect*, any *restriction* of the subject matter and the *instruction*.)

You will notice that this is a two-part question. The first part. ('What is DDT?') requires a definition paragraph, as practised on pp. 38 and 39. The second part of the question expects you to examine the statement that 'DDT contributes to human progress'. This part is deliberately wide in scope (i.e. 'human progress' can cover a large number of matters). In essence, however, the examiner wants you to tell him about the good and bad consequences of DDT.

Write an answer to this question. You may wish to base your answer on the following structure:

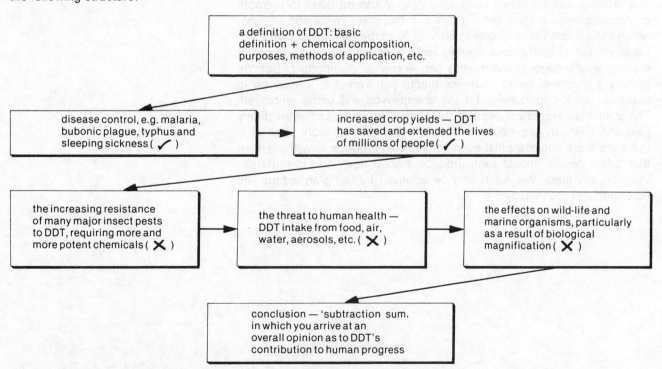

Please note that this structure only suggests *in outline* a possible approach to the question. *You will need to refer to books in the library for information to put into your answer.* Most of the information is available in encyclopaedias, but you may need to use the library catalogues to find books on DDT, malaria, crops, etc. Don't forget to use the List of Contents and the Index to speed up your search.

Unit four: Intermediate technology

Study Reading

The need for intermediate technology

In many places in the world today, the poor are getting poorer while the rich are getting richer, and the programmes of development planning and foreign aid appear to be unable to reverse[1] this trend[2]. Nearly all the developing countries have a modern sector[3], where the patterns of living
5 and working are similar to those in developed countries. But they also have a *non*-modern sector, where the patterns of living and working are not only unsatisfactory, but in many cases are even getting worse.

What is the typical condition of the poor in developing countries? Their work opportunities are so limited that they cannot work their way out of
10 their situation[4]. They are underemployed[5], or totally *un*employed[5]; when they do find occasional work their productivity[6] is extremely low. Some of them have land, but often too little land. Many[7] have no land, and no prospect of ever getting any. There is no hope for them in the rural areas, and so they drift into the big cities. But there is no work for them in the
15 big cities either – and of course no housing. All the same[8], they flock[9] into the cities because their chances of finding *some* work appear to be greater there than in the villages – where they[10] are nil. Rural unemployment, then[11], produces mass-migration into the cities; rural unemployment becomes urban unemployment.

20 The problem can be stated quite simply: what can be done to promote economic growth outside the big cities, in the small towns and villages, which still contain (in most cases) 80 to 90% of the total population? The primary need is workplaces, literally millions of workplaces. No-one, of course, would suggest that output per worker is unimportant. But the
25 primary aim cannot be to maximise output per worker[12]; it must be to maximise work opportunities for the unemployed and under-employed. The poor man's greatest need is the chance to work, and even poorly paid and relatively unproductive work is better than no work at all. It is therefore more important that everybody should produce something, than
30 that a few people should each produce a great deal. And in most developing countries, this[13] can only be achieved by using an appropriate (intermediate) technology.

Study reading questions

1 Think of *return* and a traffic di*version*. What does *reverse* mean?

2 *Which* trend?

3 Think of the words *section* and bi*sect*. We also talk of *the private sector and the public sector*. What is a *sector*, and in what context is it usually used?

4 What *is* 'their situation'?

5 What is the difference between being *underemployed* and being *unemployed*?

6 *Productivity* is concerned with producing things. The context of productivity is work, and we are told that the productivity of the poor in developing countries is low. Therefore, what does *productivity* mean?

7 *Who* or *what*?

8 Which symbol best expresses the meaning of *all the same*:
   a) ·̇
   b) ( )
   c) →

9 We talk of a *flock* of sheep, or a *flock* of goats. Therefore, what do people do when they '*flock* into the cities'?

10 *What*?

11 Which one of the following signpost words means almost the same as *then*:

   a)   in addition   +
   b)   however   →↘
   c)   therefore   ·̇

   With this meaning, what do you notice about the position of *then* in the sentence, and its punctuation? (Look at another example on p. 32, last paragraph, first sentence.)

12 The semi-colon (;) occurs twice in paragraph 2, and once in paragraph 3. The semi-colon expresses a special relationship between the two halves of the sentence. Study the three sentences, then say what that relationship is.

13 *What*?

Discussion questions

A   What are the topics of these three paragraphs:

PARAGRAPH 1 (STATEMENT OF PROBLEM)
   a)   Developing countries have both a modern and a non-modern sector.
   b)   People living in the non-modern sectors of many developing countries are becoming increasingly poor.
   c)   Programmes of development planning and foreign aid are a failure in many developing countries.

PARAGRAPH 2 (REASON)
   a)   This is because the poor in developing countries migrate to the cities.
   b)   This is because the poor in developing countries lack work opportunities.
   c)   This is because the poor in developing countries have no land.

PARAGRAPH 3 (SOLUTION)
   a)   It is therefore necessary to increase productivity.
   b)   It is therefore necessary to provide millions of workplaces in the small towns and villages.
   c)   It is therefore necessary for everybody to produce something.

Read the three topics you have chosen, one after the other. They should interconnect in meaning. *Do* they?

Essentially[14], technology can be classified into simple, intermediate and advanced:

a) Simple technology
Farmers clearing land – the simplest tools cost little to buy and nothing to operate, but the work is hard and slow and produces the least of any technology.

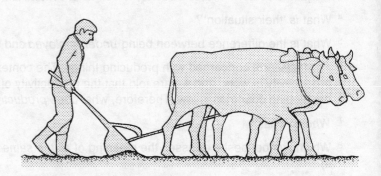

b) Intermediate technology
A farmer tilling[15] land using a wooden-shared[16] plough[17] – the tool makes the work easier, costs little and can be made locally, but a plough drawn by animals is not as productive as mechanised equipment.

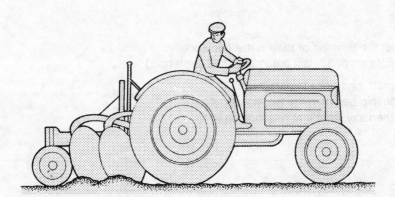

c) Advanced technology
One farmworker learns from another how to operate a modern tractor – the machinery is quick and efficient, but is expensive to buy and maintain, may deprive[18] people of work and be ecologically harmful[19].

35 There have been many cases of countries adopting advanced technology in which the results proved disastrous[20] in terms of[21] employment and foreign exchange. For example, in one poor country, 5000 shoemakers were kept very busy by their customers. Many other people earned their living by supplying material to the shoemakers: leather, handtools, cotton
40 laces, wooden lasts[22], and cartons[23]. The country then imported two plastic-injection moulding machines[24], costing over US $60 000. All the PVC for making the shoes was also imported, which meant more spending outside the country. The plastic shoes were cheaper than the leather ones, and outlasted them, and so most of the 5000 shoemakers soon
45 found themselves out of a job. So[25] did most of their suppliers. The plastic shoe factory, on the other hand, employed only 40 people.

Study reading questions

14 The signpost word *essentially* is similar in meaning to *to summarise*, but there is a difference. What is it?

15 Use the whole context (picture + words) to work out the meaning of *tilling* land.

16 A *wooden-shared* plough means that the . . . of the plough are made of . . . Which part of the plough is the share? (Think of *sharing* expenses or *sharing* a profit, and study the diagram.)

17 Use your dictionary to check the pronunciation of this word, and write its transcription.

18 Use the context to work out the meaning of *deprive*.

19 *What* (may) be ecologically harmful?

20 Read the results of adopting advanced technology in the case of making shoes. Can you now say what *disastrous* means?

21 *In terms of* explains
   a)   why
   b)   for how many people
   c)   in which areas of the economy
   the results were disastrous.

22 Picture something wooden that the shoemaker uses in his job. Can you now say what a *last* is?

23 Think of a cigarette *carton*. What does a *shoemaker* use cartons for?

24 Are these:
   a)   injection moulding machines that are made of plastic?
   b)   machines that use moulds for the injection of plastic?
   c)   plastic moulds that are injected into a machine?

25 What happened to most of the shoemakers' suppliers?

Discussion questions

B   Copy and complete:

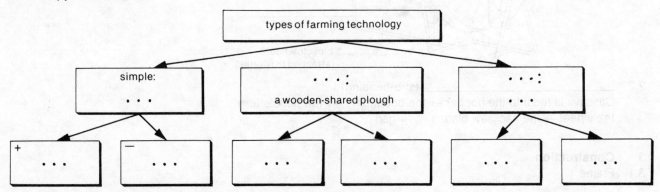

C   Can you suggest an intermediate technology for the shoe industry? What would its advantages be over the former system and the one that replaced it? Would there be any disadvantages?

D   Find words or phrases that can be replaced by the following:
damage the environment
supported themselves
lasted longer
by comparison

Making Notes from a Talk

You can greatly speed up your note-making by using *symbols*, e.g.

∴	therefore	↑	up, increase
⇒	results in, causes	↓	down, decrease
&	and	/	per, each
>	more than	%	per cent
≯	is not more than	=	equals, means
<	less than	≠	does not equal, does not mean
≮	is not less than	≡	is exactly the same as
±	plus or minus	≃	is approximately the same as

From now on, use symbols in your note-making wherever possible.

You will hear a short talk about a particular example of intermediate technology. As you listen, copy and complete the notes and diagrams. Give your notes a suitable heading and sub-headings when you have finished.

_____ (heading)

1   Existing methods of converting cassava into gari
1.1   Domestic motorised machines – too expensive (US $400–500)
1.2   Manual grinding – ...
1.3   ...

2   The 'bicycle grinder' – components and operation
(designed by the late Will Eaves at Intermediate Technology Workshop, Zaria)
2.1   Components

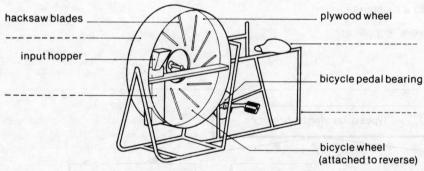

hacksaw blades _____

- - - - - - - - - - -

input hopper _____

- - - - - - - - -

plywood wheel

- - - - - - - -

bicycle pedal bearing

- - - - - - - - -

bicycle wheel
(attached to reverse)

2.2   _____ (sub-heading)
Cassava is fed into the hopper → the operator ... → the pedals turn
the wheel → the hacksaw blades ... → gari ...

3   Construction
3.1   Frame

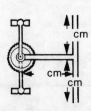 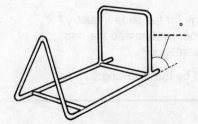 

Holds ... – made of 4 cm galvanised ...   Holds ... and the bicycle pedal bearing

3.2 Wheel
Cut from . . ., . . . in diameter, fitted with . . . The
wheel is cut open in the centre, and . . .

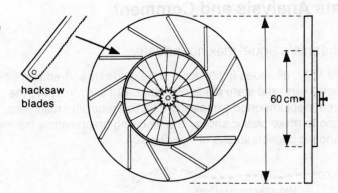

hacksaw
blades

60 cm

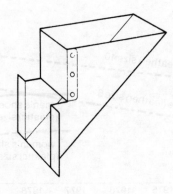

3.3 Input hopper and delivery chute
Cut from . . ., bent into shape, and riveted or
brazed together. The delivery chute also . . .,
screwed on to . . .

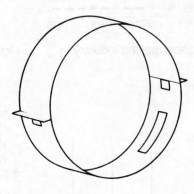

3.4 Guard
Two . . ., cut and bent . . .

4 _____ (sub-heading)
4.1 The parts of the frame are welded together.
4.2 The top guard . . .
4.3 . . . is welded to one side of the frame.
4.4 The delivery chute is screwed on to the frame.
4.5 The bottom guard . . .
4.6 The grinding wheel . . .
4.7 . . . connects . . .
4.8 . . .
4.9 The welded areas . . .
4.10 . . .

You heard the following *colloquial expressions*. What did they mean?

1 '. . . this machine costs from 400 to 500 US dollars, so it's out of the
question for the ordinary family.' (What is the meaning of *it's out of
the question*?)

2 'Not surprisingly, therefore, most people take the easy way out and
buy their gari after the cassava has been ground commercially'.
(What do you do when you *take the easy way out*?)

3 'Because it uses bicycle components, there are no prizes for
guessing what it's called!' (Why are there *no prizes for guessing
what it's called*?)

Data Analysis and Comment

Mindonia's shoe-making industry

Until 1977, all shoes in Mindonia were made by self-employed shoemakers, and were made of leather. But early in 1977, the government imported two plastic-injection moulding machines, and began to make plastic shoes. The following graphs show the major economic consequences of that decision.

Fig. 4.1 Employment in the shoe-making industry in Mindonia 1973–79

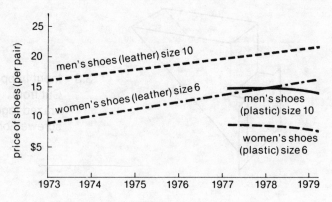

Fig. 4.2 Shoe prices in Mindonia 1973–79

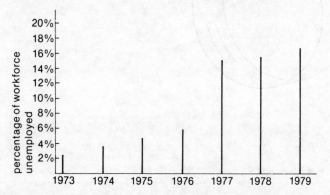

Fig. 4.3 National unemployment rates in Mindonia 1973–79

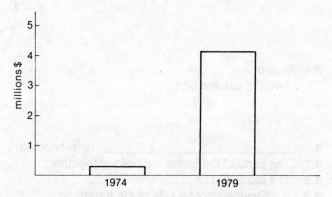

Fig. 4.4 Mindonian foreign exchange spent on importing materials for the production of shoes 1974 and 1979

Use data above to answer the following questions. Your answers will form a five-paragraph text.

Until 1977, what were shoes in Mindonia made of, and how was the shoe-making industry organised? (Until 1977, . . .) What happened in 1977? (But in 1977, . . .) What has been the general economic consequence since then? (. . . serious economic consequences.)

Contrast the number of shoemakers (leather) in 1979 with 1974. (For example, . . . in contrast to . . .) Contrast the number of workers employed in support industries – i.e. leather, handtools, cotton laces, wooden lasts, cartons, etc. – in 1979 with 1974. (Furthermore, . . . compared with . . .) How many workers were employed by the plastic shoe factory in 1979? (On the other hand, . . .) Did these figures for the shoe-making industry contribute to the increase in Mindonia's unemployment rate? (These figures . . .) Contrast the 1979 unemployment rate with the 1974 rate. (In consequence, . . . whereas . . .)

Contrast Mindonia's spending of foreign exchange on importing materials for the production of shoes in 1979, with 1974. (Mindonia spent..., as opposed to...in 1974.) What was the reason for this increase? (The reason...)

In general, were plastic shoes cheaper in 1979, than leather shoes in 1974? (In general,...) Give an example for men's shoes. (Men's plastic shoes size 10, for example,..., whereas...) Give an example for women's shoes. (And women's plastic shoes size 6..., while...)

Summarise the major 1979: 1974 contrasts mentioned above. (In sum,...)

Grammar Revision

In the following passage, ONE word has been omitted from each complete line. Copy the passage, adding the words that you think have been left out, e.g.

The People's Republic of China <u>has</u> a huge population of over 970 million. The cost <u>of</u> providing Western-style health services throughout the country <u>would</u> therefore be enormous.

China's health care system

The People's Republic of China a huge population of over
970 million. The cost providing Western-style health services
throughout the country therefore be enormous. And so in order
to provide health services that are available all and appropriate
to the needs of the majority, China created a system that lays
great stress on preventive opposed to curative care. Manpower
in China is plentiful, capital is. Thus the system rests on
labour-intensive methods and employs very numbers of community
health workers ('barefoot doctors').

It was 1965 – during the Cultural Revolution – that the
'barefoot doctor' emerged. His role in the health services poor
rural regions makes him a model for sort of medical auxiliaries
needed in the developing world. In community in China there is
a 'barefoot doctor', trained practical experience gained
by working mobile health teams, through observation and
instruction. Essentially, the 'barefoot doctor's' duties to
diagnose and treat simple ailments, to educate community on
preventive care, and to organise the vaccination members of
the community.

Writing A Set of Instructions

1 Introduction – How to write a set of instructions

Earlier in this unit, you completed notes on the assembly of the bicycle cassava grinder. Your completed notes were probably similar to:

1   The parts of the frame are welded together.
2   The top guard is bolted to the frame.
3   The input hopper is welded to one side of the frame.
4   The delivery chute is screwed on to the frame under the hopper.
5   The bottom guard is screwed to the top guard.
6   The grinding wheel is fixed on to brackets by means of nuts.
7   A chain connects the wheel and pedal cogs.
8   The seat is bolted to the frame.
9   The welded areas are cleaned.
10 The machine is painted.

If you were writing a set of instructions, telling someone how to assemble the cassava grinder, your instructions would look like this:

1   Weld the parts of the frame together.
2   Bolt the top guard to the frame.
3   Weld the input hopper to one side of the frame.
4   Screw...
5   ...
6   ...
7   ...
8   ...
9   ...
10 ...

You will notice the following characteristics about this set of instructions:

— Each instruction is numbered.

— There is only *one* instruction per number.

— Instructions are written in the exact order of performance.

— Instructions are short and uncomplicated, but grammatically complete.

— The imperative form of the most appropriate 'activity' verb (*weld, bolt, screw*...) is used, preferably the first word of each instruction.

also — Annotated line drawings or photographs usually accompany instructions.

— Drawings or photographs are integrated with the text by reference to the appropriate figure number.

Complete the instructions for assembling the cassava grinder.

2 A set of instructions for building an iceless cooler

In a warm climate, perishable food has to be kept as cool as possible, to keep it fresh and to prevent spoilage. However, electric or gas refrigerators are expensive for a family in a developing country, and electricity or gas is often not available in rural areas. An 'intermediate technology' answer is an iceless cooler, which can be constructed very cheaply using local materials.

The following is a description of how such a cooler was made. Rewrite the description into a set of instructions for construction, incorporating the diagram into your instructions.

> The first thing we had to do was to select a cool place in the kitchen, away from the stove, then we placed the outer container there. Bricks or stones were arranged in the container so that the basket would balance evenly on them. We sewed canvas around the rim of the basket, and let it hang loosely around the bottom and extend into the earthenware or metal container. The basket was set on the bricks, but before that we sewed canvas loosely over the cover of the basket. Then the cover was put on, and food was placed in the basket. The next step was to put water in the bottom of the container. Of course, we had to make sure the basket was not standing in water. (The canvas cover hangs down into the water and absorbs it, with the result that the food inside the basket stays cool.)

You should check that your instructions are in the correct order. Also, the information in brackets will *not* form part of your instructions.

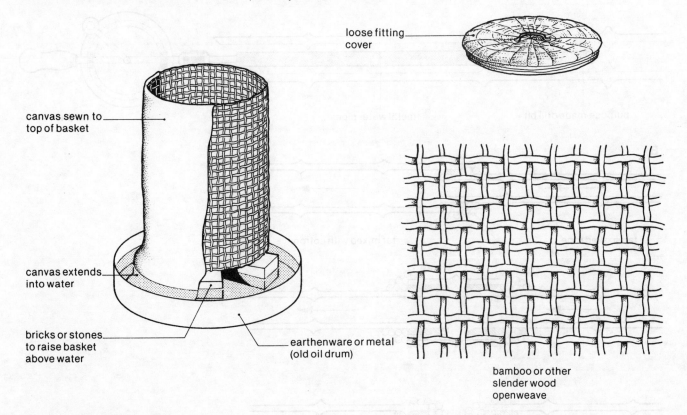

loose fitting cover

canvas sewn to top of basket

canvas extends into water

bricks or stones to raise basket above water

earthenware or metal (old oil drum)

bamboo or other slender wood openweave

Fig. 4.5 An iceless cooler

Text Completion

Complete the following text by writing suitable sentences that may be
added in places (A) and (B). You will probably need to write two or three
sentences for (A), and three or four for (B). The diagrams provide the
information required.

Bamboo water pipes

Piped water from a river, spring or well is extremely important for
irrigation purposes. For some developing countries, however, metal
piping is expensive. Therefore, in countries where bamboo is readily
available, it can be used as water piping material where the flow is under
gravity.

In preparing bamboo for water piping, the first step is to remove the
inter-nodes that are found every 30–80 cm along the bamboo stem, as
they interrupt the flow. One way . . . (A) . . . Another way . . .

There are several ways of jointing the bamboo sections. The first is
to . . . (B) . . .

(A)

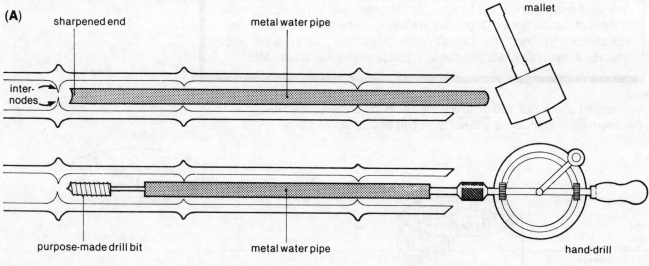

(B)

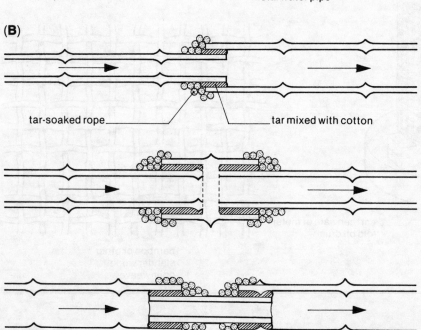

Writing Examination Answers

The instruction *contrast* (= *distinguish between*)

A dictionary definition of *contrast*: 'to show the differences between'

Contrast or *Distinguish between* questions usually present you with two or more terms, instruments, concepts or procedures that are closely connected, and sometimes confused. The examiner wants to know whether you can explain the differences between them. Note that you are only required to show how they are *different*; you are *not* required to show how they are the same.

The way you organise your answer will depend on what you are being asked, but a suitable answer structure would be:

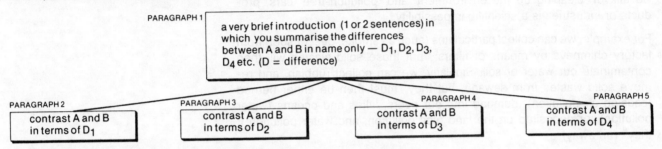

PARAGRAPH 1
a very brief introduction (1 or 2 sentences) in which you summarise the differences between A and B in name only — D₁, D₂, D₃, D₄ etc. (D = difference)

PARAGRAPH 2
contrast A and B in terms of D₁

PARAGRAPH 3
contrast A and B in terms of D₂

PARAGRAPH 4
contrast A and B in terms of D₃

PARAGRAPH 5
contrast A and B in terms of D₄

You will notice that this examination answer structure does not include a conclusion paragraph, since you are *not* asked to choose between A and B.

Consider the following examination question:

Distinguish between simple, intermediate and advanced technology in ploughing land.

(What is the *subject matter* of this question? Is there a *restriction* of the subject matter? Is there an *aspect*?)

In answering this question, the diagrams on p. 44 will start you thinking. A possible answer structure is:

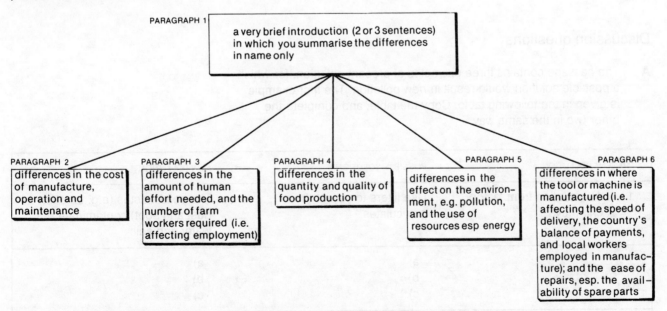

PARAGRAPH 1
a very brief introduction (2 or 3 sentences) in which you summarise the differences in name only

PARAGRAPH 2
differences in the cost of manufacture, operation and maintenance

PARAGRAPH 3
differences in the amount of human effort needed, and the number of farm workers required (i.e. affecting employment)

PARAGRAPH 4
differences in the quantity and quality of food production

PARAGRAPH 5
differences in the effect on the environment, e.g. pollution, and the use of resources esp energy

PARAGRAPH 6
differences in where the tool or machine is manufactured (i.e. affecting the speed of delivery, the country's balance of payments, and local workers employed in manufacture); and the ease of repairs, esp. the availability of spare parts

Now write an answer to this question. In your answer, use the *contrast* expressions you used in the Data Analysis passage on pp. 48 and 49. Which words in paragraphs 2–6 will you <u>underline</u> in your answer?

Unit five: Pollution

Study Reading

Everything must go somewhere

To maintain[1] his standards of living, 20th century man employs technology[2] to produce an enormous variety of goods and services. Technology needs energy and matter. But energy and matter can be neither created nor destroyed, only transformed[3]. And since everything
5 must go somewhere, the transformations which are part of production processes cause[4] pollution in some form or other – this[5] is unavoidable. So talk of 'cleaning up the environment' and 'pollution-free' cars, products or industries is a scientific impossibility.

For example, we can collect particulates (such as smoke, dust or soot) from
10 factory chimneys by means of filters[6], but these solid wastes will then contaminate our water or soil. Similarly, we can collect rubbish, and remove solid wastes from sewage, but they[7] must then be either burned (causing air pollution), dumped into our rivers, lakes and oceans (water pollution), or deposited on the land (soil pollution, and water pollution if
15 they[8] run away).

Another example is air pollution from cars. We can reduce air pollution from petrol- and diesel-propelled cars by changing over to electric cars. But electric cars would need to have their batteries recharged[9] almost every night, and so we should need to increase the number of power
20 plants to generate the extra electricity required. And an increase in the number of power plants that use fossil fuels would result in increased air pollution (from sulphur oxides, nitrogen oxide and smoke), increased water pollution (from heat), and increased land pollution (from mining). We can[10] shift[11] to nuclear power, which is not dependent on fossil fuels. But
25 nuclear power increases thermal[12] pollution of the water, and adds the danger of releasing radioactive substances into the environment.

Discussion questions

A The passage contains three examples of present pollution, for which a possible solution would result in *new* pollution. The first example is given in the following table. Copy the table, and complete the other two in the same way.

PRESENT POLLUTION	→	POSSIBLE SOLUTION	→	NEW POLLUTION
1 Air pollution from factory chimneys	→	Use filters to collect the particulates.	→	The solid wastes (e.g. smoke, dust and soot) contaminate our water and soil.
2	⇕	a) b) c)	⇕	a) b) c)
3	⇗	a) b)	⇗	a) b)

Study reading questions

1 Use your dictionary to find the noun which corresponds to the verb *to maintain*. (Mark the stress in both words.)

2 Use your dictionary to find the noun describing a person and the adjective which corresponds to the noun *technology*. (Mark the stress in all three words.)

3 Think of *trans*late (i.e. *from* one language *to* another), and different *forms* of government. What does *transformed* mean?

4 *What* cause pollution in some form or other? (Answer in one word.)

5 *What* is unavoidable?

6 The context tells us that *filters* collect the solid waste particulates (e.g. smoke, dust or soot) from factory chimneys. What goes out of the factory chimneys into the atmosphere? Therefore, draw a simple *filter*.

7 *What* must be burned; dumped into rivers, lakes or oceans; or deposited on the land?

8 If *what* run away? Where to?

9 The context tells us that the *batteries* of *electric cars* would have to be *recharged* almost every night. Think also of the meaning of *re* as in *re*vise and *re*new. Therefore, what does *recharge* mean?

10 Why is the word *can* italicised?

11 The passage mentions *shifting* from fossil fuel power plants *to* nuclear power plants. What is the meaning of *shift*?

12 Consider a *therm*ometer. What does *thermal* mean?

Discussion questions

B Consider the three examples of pollution mentioned in (**A**). Can you think of possible solutions that a) cause *no* pollution; or b) cause the least possible pollution?

C Now think of two other instances of pollution *not* mentioned in the passage, and add them to the table in (**A**) (Present Pollution → Possible Solution → New Pollution).

D What is the meaning of the phrase *everything must go somewhere*? This phrase occurs four times in the passage (the heading, the first paragraph, and twice in the final paragraph). What is the purpose and the effect of this?

From these examples it can be seen that pollution elimination[13] is impossible. Instead[14], our aim must be pollution reduction and control. One means of doing this[15] is to make the best possible use of technology. In fact[16], technology is essential in keeping pollution below the danger level.
30 However, pollution control alone is not enough. It must be accompanied by population control, and control over production and consumption. The reason is that there is no point in controlling pollution without at the same time stabilising[17] world population, production of goods, and consumption
35 of materials. But if we tackle[18] all these matters[19] at the same time, pollution control is possible.

Time is running out[20], however. Everything must go somewhere, and so pollution is beginning to have serious effects. Already many of the world's rivers and lakes are devoid[21] of marine life — killed by industrial waste.
40 Already the amount of lead in the bodies of people living in urban areas is dangerously high[22], because of car exhaust gases. Already the hearing of millions of factory workers is irreparably[23] damaged, as a result of industrial noise. Everything must go somewhere — yes. But it is for man to decide how much pollution he creates, what form it takes, and where it goes.

Study reading questions

13 The previous two paragraphs give examples of pollution, and show that the *elimination* of pollution is impossible. Using the context of these examples, work out the meaning of *elimination*.

14 Do you think that the symbol ⮌ expresses the function of the signpost word *Instead*? If so, why? If not, why not?

15 Doing *what*?

16 Complete the following to show the two pieces of information linked by the signpost word *In fact*:
    Use technology to reduce
    and control pollution ▷►○ To be safe from pollution, ...

17 Using the context, does *stabilising* mean
    a)   increasing?
    b)   decreasing?
    c)   keeping at the same amount?

18 The context of *tackle* is *problems*. Consider also the word *attack*. What do we do with problems before we solve them, i.e. what is the meaning of *tackle*?

19 *Which* matters?

20 Consider also *running out of food*, and *our money is running out*. What is happening when *Time is running out*?

21 The context tells us that marine life has been killed by industrial waste in many lakes and rivers. As a result, they are now *devoid* of marine life. Therefore, what does *devoid* mean?

22 *What* is dangerously high? (Give the extended subject, then its principal noun.)

23 Use word analysis to work out the meaning of ir/repar/ably. Use your dictionary to mark the stress in *irreparably*.

Discussion questions

E   Suggest examples of using technology to reduce and control pollution. How effective are the examples that you suggest, and can you think of improvements?

F   *Why* is there '...no point in controlling pollution without at the same time stabilising world population, production of goods, and consumption of materials'?

G   What is the effect of using the word *already* three times in the final paragraph? What is the effect of making it the first word in the sentence?

H   Find words or phrases that can be replaced by the following:
insufficient
go together with
This is because
simultaneously

Making Notes from a Talk

Word omissions and abbreviations

Word *omissions* mean leaving out unimportant words when writing notes. For example, the sentence *We can discourage the use of cars* can be written in your notes as *Discourage use cars*. Similarly, the sentence *We are trying to control the emissions from the engine* can be written in note-form as *Trying control engine emissions*.

Word *abbreviations* leave out unimportant letters from words, e.g.
discourage becomes disc
control .... cntrl
engine .... eng
emissions .... emsns

Our two sentences can now be written in note-form as *Disc use cars*, and *Trying cntrl eng emsns*.

Using word omissions and word abbreviations in your note-making will certainly save you time. But you should only use this technique if you are *sure you can later understand what you have written*. It is not important whether anyone else can understand your notes, but it is most important that *you* can.

You will hear a short talk about a certain pollution problem. As you listen, copy and complete the notes and diagrams. Give your notes a suitable heading and sub-headings when you have finished.

_____ (heading)

1   Sources of air pollution in a city

industry —17%
power plants —14%
heating and/or air conditioning —6%
waste disposal —3%

(in some cities, the car causes ... % of all air pollution)

2   _____ (sub-heading)

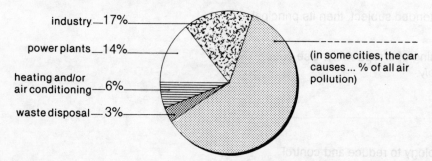

carburettor and fuel tank evaporation
...% of the hydrocarbons

noise and heat

heat

... particles (from brakes)

... particles (from tyres)

exhaust
100% of the carbon monoxide
... % of the nitrogen oxides
... % of the ...
... % of the hydrocarbons

crankcase blowby
... % of the hydrocarbons

3 Ways of controlling/reducing air pollution from cars

3.1 Discourage the use of cars – ...

3.2 ...

3.3 Use alternative fuels ...

3.4 ...

3.5 Control emissions from the engine, e.g. a catalytic converter –

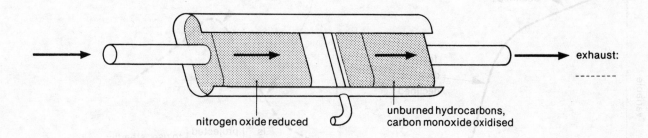

nitrogen oxide reduced

unburned hydrocarbons,
carbon monoxide oxidised

exhaust:

The catalyst removes ... from the ... and combines it with unburned ....
and ... The end-products are ... (all relatively harmless).

You heard the following *markers* in the talk. What was their significance?

1 'As you've probably already guessed, our topic today is the car. In particular, ...' (What *type* of information follows the marker *in particular*? Do you remember the specific information in the talk?)

2 'Let's take the exhaust ...' (What does the marker *Let's take X* tell you?)

3 'So – let's focus our attention now on ways of controlling or reducing the amount of air pollution caused by the car.' (What happens when you *focus your attention* on X? Think what happens when you focus the lens of your camera.)

You heard the following *colloquial expressions*. What did they mean?

4 'But perhaps the machine that the man-in-the-street is most familiar with is the car.' (Who is *the man-in-the-street*?)

5 'This is the situation, then, and it's going to get much worse – unless we use our grey matter to do something about it.' (What is our *grey matter*?)

6 'As I'm sure you can see, there are problems with each of these ways; but at least they're a step in the right direction.' (What is *a step in the right direction*?)

What did the following items of *formal vocabulary* mean?

7 '... if you look at this pie-chart, you'll see a *breakdown* of the major sources of air pollution in a typical city.'

8 'What happens is that the car's internal combustion engine is a kind of chemical factory on *a small scale*.'

9 'The *end-products* are water, carbon dioxide and nitrogen – all relatively harmless.'

10 'Probably the best answer is a *synthesis* of all five.'

Data Analysis and Comment

Study the following vocabulary connected with graphs:

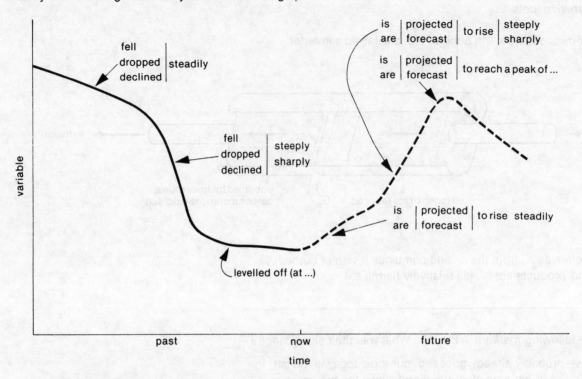

1 Now study Fig. 5.1 and answer the questions below it to form an accompanying text. The answer fragments in brackets will help you.

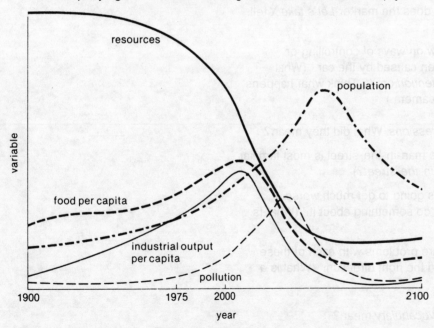

Fig. 5.1 Projections for the 21st century

What relationship and projections does Fig. 5.1 show? (Fig. 5.1 shows ... between ... from 1900 to the present day, and projections ...)

Comment on the data for resources. (Resources ... to the present day, and are projected to ...) Comment on pollution and population. (..., and are forecast to ...) Comment on food and industrial output per capita. (..., and are projected to ...)

Why are population and pollution forecast to continue to grow after the peak of industrialisation? (It is forecast that ... because ...) Why is a sharp decline in population projected to start in the middle of the 21st century? (... reduced medical services and food.) Why is pollution forecast to drop sharply from about 2030? (Similarly, ...)

How can the projected disaster in the 21st century be averted? (One means of averting ... is to ... Another means is to ...)

In the text that you have just completed, in which order did the following paragraph topics appear?
Explanation of the data
Possible solutions
The major trends
Introduction

2 Write a five-paragraph text in which you analyse and comment on the following graph. Your five paragraphs should have the topics:

1 Introduction – what the graph shows
2 General trends
3 Levels for smokers aged 30–50, and projections for smokers aged 51–70
4 Levels for non-smokers aged 30–50, and projections for non-smokers aged 51–70
5 Possible solutions

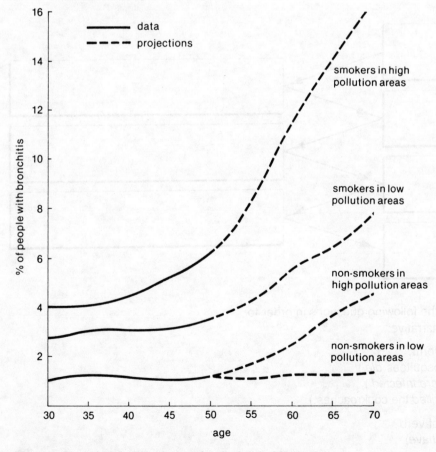

Fig. 5.2 Bronchitis*, smoking and pollution in Mindonia.

---

* Bronchitis is an illness in which the lining of the pipes in the lungs is very sore, so that a person has a bad cough, a high temperature and breathing problems.

Writing a Narrative

1   Read the following:

Malaria at one time infected 90% of the population of Borneo. In 1955,
the World Health Organisation began a DDT spraying programme which
virtually eliminated malaria. But other things began to happen. Besides
killing mosquitoes, the DDT also killed other insects that lived in the
houses, such as flies and cockroaches. These insects were the favourite
food of geckos (small lizards). And so when the geckos ate the
dead insects, they died from DDT poisoning. Similarly, the house cats ate
the dead geckos and cockroaches, and they too died from DDT
poisoning. As a result, the rat population rose sharply, and the human
population of Borneo began to die from a type of plague carried by fleas
on the rats. In order to deal with the emergency, thousands of cats were
parachuted into the island, in what was called 'Operation Cat Drop'.

This passage is a *narrative*, i.e. it outlines a sequence of steps carried out
on a specific occasion. Narrative is particularly important in report-writing,
when the writer outlines the developmental stages of an experiment or a
piece of research, or the sequence of steps in an event such as a fire or
an accident.

Identify the stages in the DDT sequence above, by completing the
note-form summary:

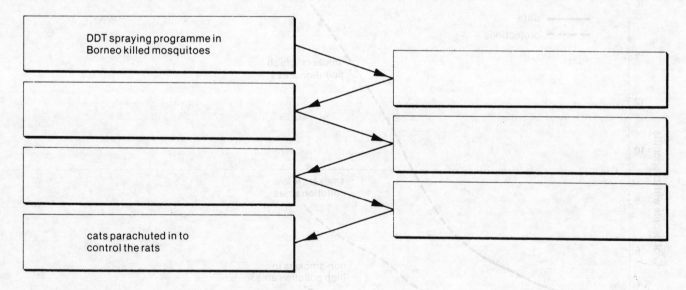

Read the narrative again, then answer the following questions in order to
identify the characteristics of writing a narrative:

1   Which is the most common verb form:
   a)   simple present (e.g. The mosquitoes *die*.)
   b)   passive (e.g. The geckos *were infected*.)
   c)   simple past (e.g. The DDT *killed* the cockroaches.)

2   Which is the most common type of verb?
   a)   stative (e.g. *were, became, have*)
   b)   active (e.g. *killed, rose*)

3   Is the sequence of steps
   a)   in the exact order in which they took place?
   b)   in a random order?

2 Study the following table. It sets out the main stages in an incident that took place in 1967, in which an oil tanker caused widespread pollution. Use the information in the table to write the introduction to a report on the incident. You will be writing a *narrative*.

DESCRIPTION OF SHIP

name	type	dead-weight tonnage	length	importance
Torrey Canyon	oil tanker	118 000 tonnes	355 m	one of the largest tankers afloat at the time

SEQUENCE OF EVENTS

date	event	direct result	environmental consequence	action
18.3.67	'Torrey Canyon' / Seven Stones Reef (off S.W. coast of England)	cargo tanks / holes	S.W. coastline / oil pollution	attempts to refloat tanker were unsuccessful
22.3.67	engine room (explosion)	salvage chief		
27.3.67		thousands more tonnes of oil		
28.3.67		40 000 tonnes of oil gushed into the sea	S.W. coastline / more pollution	Barracuda Oil Co. (ship's owners) Set fire to the oil
29.3.67		2 km	smoke 1000 m	

Grammar Revision

In the following passage, ONE word has been omitted from each complete line. Copy the passage, adding words that you think have been left out, e.g.

Many industrial plants – <u>especially</u> fossil fuel and nuclear power
plants – withdraw water <u>from</u> a lake or river for cooling purposes.

Thermal water pollution

Many industrial plants – fossil fuel and nuclear power
plants – withdraw water a lake or river for cooling
purposes. The water returned to its source, but
at a high temperature that thermal pollution takes place.
As a result, several undesirable ecological changes place
in the lake or river. One of changes is known as thermal
shock, aquatic life is suddenly killed because of a sharp
increase temperature. Also, the migration patterns of certain species
disrupted. And the food chain is also disrupted the loss of one or
more key species (especially plankton) at lower levels the food
chain. Finally, some species become more susceptible parasites,
chemical toxins, and disease.

Text Completion

Complete the following text by writing suitable sentences that may be added in spaces (A) and (B). You will probably need to write three or four sentences in each place. The diagrams provide the information required.

Water pollution control

There are several ways of dealing with a society's liquid wastes. They can be dumped into the nearest waterway, they can be treated by means of septic tanks or sewage treatment plants, or the valuable nutrients in liquid waste can be recycled to the land as fertilizer.

At present, the most common method involves treating liquid wastes in sewage treatment plants. In this method, ... (A) ...

But this linear system of water use is overloading our lakes and rivers with nitrate and phosphate plant nutrients, and so they are becoming increasingly polluted. Instead, we should adopt a *cyclical* system in which such nutrients would be returned to the land as fertilizer. In such a system, the water used by man would ... (B) ...

(A)

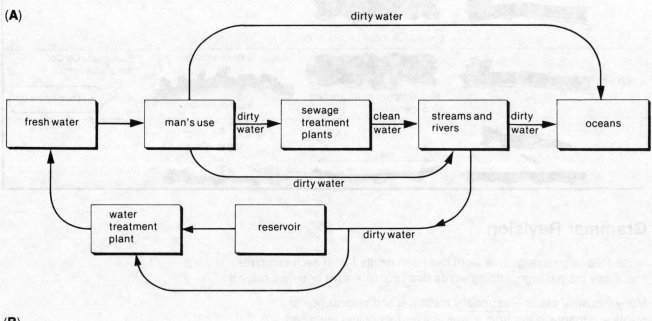

(B)

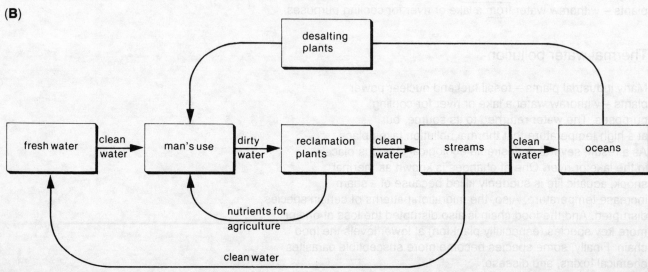

Writing Examination Answers

The instruction *to what extent*

A dictionary definition of *to what extent*: 'how far, to what degree'

Consider the following examination question:

To what extent can the major sources of noise pollution be reduced?

(Identify the *subject matter*. Is there an *aspect*, and a *restriction*, of the subject matter?)
The examiner is saying to you, in effect, 'Here is a statement: noise pollution can be reduced. It is obviously true. But truth is never 100%. *How* true is it? Are there areas where you disagree with the statement? If so, tell me how far you agree, and your points of agreement and disagreement.'

We can see this diagrammatically:

(basic statement in the question: 'Noise pollution can be reduced')

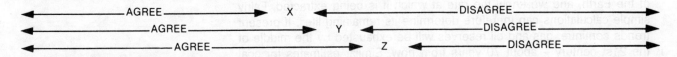

To what extent do you agree with the statement in the question? Up to point x, y or z? You must justify your points of agreement or disagreement. The extent of your agreement/disagreement is up to you, of course. But *avoid total agreement or total disagreement.* The very fact that the examiner has used the instruction *to what extent* is proof that there are two sides to the matter; the examiner therefore expects you to *show* him both sides.

Now write an answer to the question. A possible answer structure is:

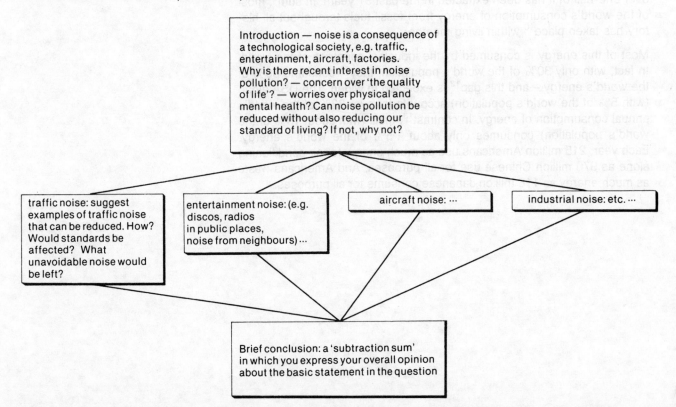

Introduction — noise is a consequence of a technological society, e.g. traffic, entertainment, aircraft, factories. Why is there recent interest in noise pollution? — concern over 'the quality of life'? — worries over physical and mental health? Can noise pollution be reduced without also reducing our standard of living? If not, why not?

traffic noise: suggest examples of traffic noise that can be reduced. How? Would standards be affected? What unavoidable noise would be left?

entertainment noise: (e.g. discos, radios in public places, noise from neighbours) ...

aircraft noise: ...

industrial noise: etc. ...

Brief conclusion: a 'subtraction sum' in which you express your overall opinion about the basic statement in the question

Unit six: Alternative sources of energy

Study Reading

The energy crisis

If present trends continue, the world will face a major crisis[1] by the end of this century: insufficient cheap, convenient energy. For without such energy, industrial production will fall, agricultural output will drop, transport will be restricted, and standards of living in developed countries will
5 plummet[2].

At present, almost all our energy comes from fossil fuels (oil, coal and natural gas). The Earth's reserves of fossil fuels have been formed from organic matter subjected to enormous heat and pressure for millions of years. But such reserves[3] are finite[4]. Because power demand is increas-
10 ing very rapidly, fossil fuels will be exhausted within a relatively short time. We can estimate the amount of recoverable fuel under the surface of the Earth, and we know the rate at which it is being extracted. Fairly simple calculations can therefore determine its remaining life[5]. If present trends continue, gas and oil reserves will be exhausted by the middle of
15 the 21st century – about 70 years from now. Similar estimates for coal reserves suggest[6] a projected supply of 250–300 years. Of course, long before fossil fuels are exhausted, demand[7] will greatly exceed supply[7].

For too many years, the world has consumed fossil fuels with little thought for the future. In fact[8], world energy consumption increased almost
20 600% between 1900 and 1965, and is projected to increase another 450% between 1965 and the year 2000. Crude oil has been pumped out of the ground for about 100 years, but over one-half of it has been consumed in the past 18 years. Coal has been mined for over 800 years, but over one-half of it has been extracted in the past 37 years. In sum[9], most
25 of the world's consumption of energy from fossil fuels throughout all history has taken place[10] within living memory.

Most of this energy is consumed by the industrial countries of the world. In fact, with only 30% of the world's population, they[11] consume 80% of the world's energy – and this gap[12] is expected to widen. The USA alone
30 (with 5% of the world's population) accounts for over 32% of the world's annual consumption of energy. In contrast[13], India (with about 15% of the world's population) consumes only about 1·5% of the world's energy. Each year, 215 million Americans use as much energy for air conditioning alone as 970 million Chinese use for all purposes. And Americans *waste*
35 as much energy as 116 million Japanese consume for all purposes.

Study reading questions

Use your dictionary to check the pronunciation of *crisis*, and write its transcription, including the stress mark.
What is the adjective? Write its transcription, including the stress mark.

2 Consider the other verbs in this sentence – *fall, drop, restricted*. With this context, what is the general meaning of *plummet*? Now consider additionally the more specific context of '... without such energy... standards of living in developed countries will plummet'. Can you suggest a more specific meaning of *plummet*?

3 *Which* reserves?

4 Consider the context of the following sentence, i.e. '... fossil fuels will be exhausted within a relatively short time.' Therefore, what is the meaning of *finite*?

5 Use your dictionary to complete: *its remaining life = the ... of its life.*

6 *What* suggest a projected fuel supply of 250–300 years? (Answer in one word.)

7 Demand for *what*? Supply of *what*?

8 Which relationship does *In fact* signpost?

a)   ◐━▶◯   general to specific
b)   ⟹   cause and effect
c)   ╋   statement plus additional statement

9 Which one of the following signpost words means approximately the same as *in sum*?
a)   in other words
b)   in essence
c)   to conclude

10 *What* has taken place within living memory? (Give the extended subject, then its principal noun.)

11 *Who* or *what*?

12 *Which* gap?

13 Suggest an appropriate symbol that illustrates the function of *In contrast*.

Discussion questions

A   The NOUN + NOUN phrase *fossil fuels* means 'fuels from fossils'. What do the following mean?
power demand
world energy consumption
coal reserves

B   Paragraph 3 outlines the consumption of oil and coal in the last 18 and 37 years respectively, in relation to the total consumption time. Draw a graph to show these facts, so as to emphasise the increased consumption in recent years.

C   Discuss ways in which energy consumption can be reduced, especially in America.

D   In paragraph 2, we are told that 'fairly simple calculations' can determine the remaining life of a fossil fuel. Assuming an average increase in consumption of 6% p.a., write an equation to determine a fossil fuel's remaining life.

In the early 1970s, the world at last woke up to the fact that fossil fuels are a precious gift of nature, and their supply is strictly limited. The considerable increase in the price of oil that occurred at this time caused[14] balance of payments problems in many oil-importing countries. As a re-
40 sult, attention has turned to the pressing problem of alternative sources of energy.

In Fig. 6.1, energy flow to and from the Earth is shown by means of bands and lines that suggest by their width their respective[15] contributions to the Earth's energy supply. The principal inputs[16] are solar radiation
45 (which accounts for more than 99%); winds, waves and currents; and the energy from nuclear, thermal and gravitational sources. Since fossil fuels are finite, scientists are now actively developing these[17] alternative sources of energy.

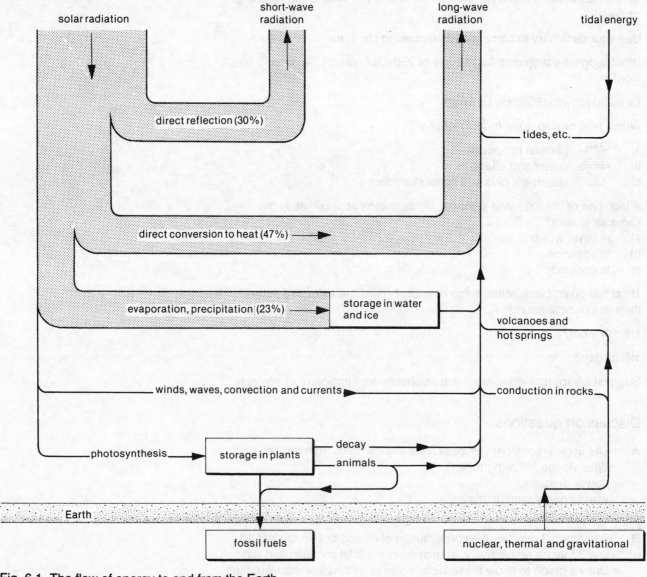

Fig. 6.1 The flow of energy to and from the Earth

The world faces, then, three immediate tasks. To extend the life of fossil
50 fuels, all countries must reduce energy waste. Industrialised countries must reduce energy consumption so that available supplies are shared out more equitably[18]. And in preparation for the time when fossil fuels run out, alternative sources of infinite, cheap, convenient energy must be developed.

Study reading questions

14 *What* caused balance of payments problems in many oil-importing countries? (Give the extended subject, then its principal noun.)

15 Fig. 6.1 indicates the contributions of direct reflection, direct conversion to heat, and evaporation and precipitation to the Earth's energy supply. Are their *respective* contributions 47%, 23% and 30%? If not, what *are* their respective contributions?

16 Analyse the word parts of *inputs* to suggest its meaning.

17 *Which* alternative sources of energy?

18 We have already seen (p. 66, paragraph 4) that industrial countries consume a disproportionately large share of the world's energy in relation to their population. We are now told that industrialised countries '... must reduce energy consumption so that available supplies are shared out more *equitably*'. Consider also the *equa*tor and an *equa*tion, then suggest the meaning of *equitably*.

Discussion questions

E   Verbalise Fig. 6.1, i.e. express its contents in speech or writing.

F   The final paragraph indicates that the world faces three tasks.
     Tabulate those tasks as follows:

ACTION	PURPOSE

G   Find words or phrases that can be replaced by the following:
     they are finite
     urgent
     conserve energy
     are exhausted

Making Notes from a Talk

You will hear a short talk about an alternative source of energy. As you listen, copy and complete the notes and diagrams.

_____ (heading)

1 _____ (sub-heading)
1.1 ...
1.2 Cleanest and safest of all energy sources
1.3 ...
1.4 ...

2 _____ (sub-heading)
2.1 ...
2.2 Not available at night (highest energy needs)
2.3 ...
2.4 Storage system needed

3 Odeillo solar power station (France)

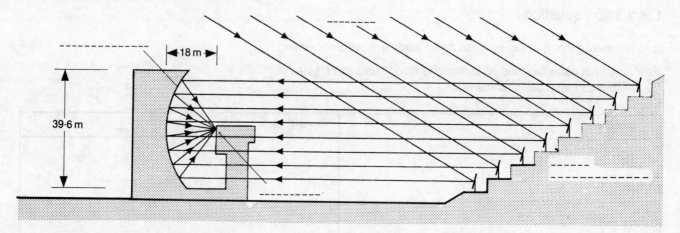

4 Satellite solar power station

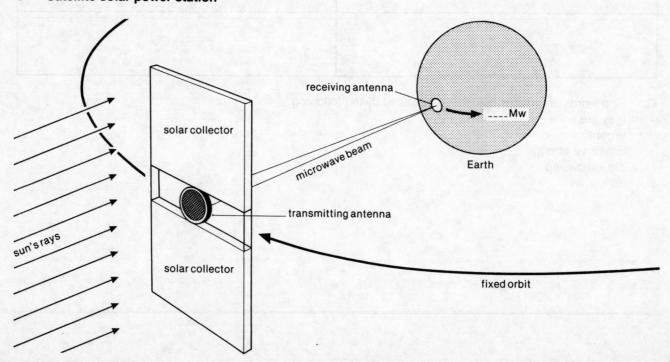

You heard the following *markers* in the talk. What was their significance?

1   'Well, what advantages does solar energy have over other energy sources?' (Which is the key word in this marker, that indicates the type of information to come?)

2   'All right, you say. With so many advantages, what's the snag? Why haven't we used the sun to solve our energy problems long ago?' (What type of information do you expect to follow? Can you sum up this type of information in one word? It can form the sub-heading for this section of your notes.)

3   'How far have we got, then, in harnessing the power of the sun?' (Which are the key words in this marker, that suggest the type of information to come?)

You heard the following *colloquial expressions*. What did they mean?

4   'All right, you say. With so many advantages, what's the snag? Why haven't we used the sun to solve our energy problems before?' (What is a *snag*?)

5   'How far have we got, then, in harnessing the power of the sun?' (A horse wears a harness. What for? Therefore, what is meant by *harnessing* the power of the sun?)

6   'The solar cells would convert the sun's radiation into electricity, which would then be fed into a microwave generator.' (*Fed into* is an (originally) colloquial phrase which is now an accepted technical term. What does it mean?)

What did the following items of *formal vocabulary* mean?

7   '. . . no major *breakthroughs* are needed to make solar energy technologically *feasible*'.

8   'These are banks of huge mirrors. They turn *automatically* to follow the sun's path . . .'

9   'One satellite of this size could *generate* 10 000 megawatts . . .'

10 'What we must do now is to *invest* very large sums of money into the necessary *research* and *development*.'

In the following extracts, the lecturer a) used an unfamiliar word and so b) explained the meaning of that word immediately it was used. Identify a) the word, and b) the explanation.

11 'In the first place, it's infinite and readily available. For example, if only 1% of the never-ending solar energy falling on the Sahara Desert could be converted to electrical power, it would supply all the world's projected energy needs for the year 2000.'

12 'First, solar energy reaching the Earth's surface is widely dispersed – spread out.'

13 'Suppose, however, that we could place the solar mirrors (called collectors) above the Earth's surface?'

Data Analysis and Comment

Study and discuss the following graphs. Then use them as the basis for writing a three-paragraph text entitled *How long will fossil fuels last?*

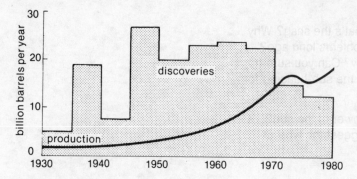

Fig. 6.2 Oil discoveries and production

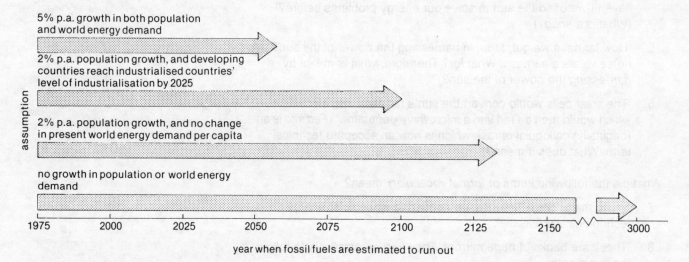

year when fossil fuels are estimated to run out

Fig. 6.3 The estimated life of fossil fuels

The following is a possible text structure:

PARAGRAPH 1: the relationship between discoveries and production:
  – the general trend of discoveries until the 1970s
  – the general trend of production until the 1970s
  – the trend in the 1970s, and its effects
  – projections for the 1980s and 1990s

PARAGRAPH 2: assuming a recovery efficiency of 100%, forecasts of the life
of fossil fuels with:
  a) 5% p.a. growth in population and world energy demand.
  b) 2% p.a. population growth, and developing countries
     reaching the industrialised countries' industrialisation
     level by 2025
  c) 2% p.a. population growth, and no change in the present
     world energy demand per capita.
  d) no growth in population or world energy demand.

PARAGRAPH 3: the importance of developing alternative energy sources

Add other comments that you consider relevant. Check your paragraph
structure – especially topic sentences, and inter-sentence and
inter-paragraph cohesion.

Text Completion

Complete the following text by writing suitable sentences that may be added in places (A) and (B). You will probably need to write three or four sentences in each place. The diagrams provide the information required.

Alternative sources of energy

Because fossil fuels are finite, a number of alternative sources of energy are currently under research. One of these is wind power. One environmental objection, however, is the 'visual pollution' of the landscape that would be caused by tall windmills, especially since they would be concentrated in areas of constant high winds.

An answer is to locate windmills in the sea. In fact, an off-shore wind energy system has recently been proposed along the north-east coast of the USA. The floating windmills would be of an unusual design. . . . (A) . . .

Another alternative source is geothermal energy. Such energy is produced when rocks lying thousands of metres below the Earth's surface are heated to high temperatures. These high temperatures result from energy produced by the decay of radioactive elements in the earth, or by non-radioactive materials such as magma or molten rock. . . . (B) . . .

(A)

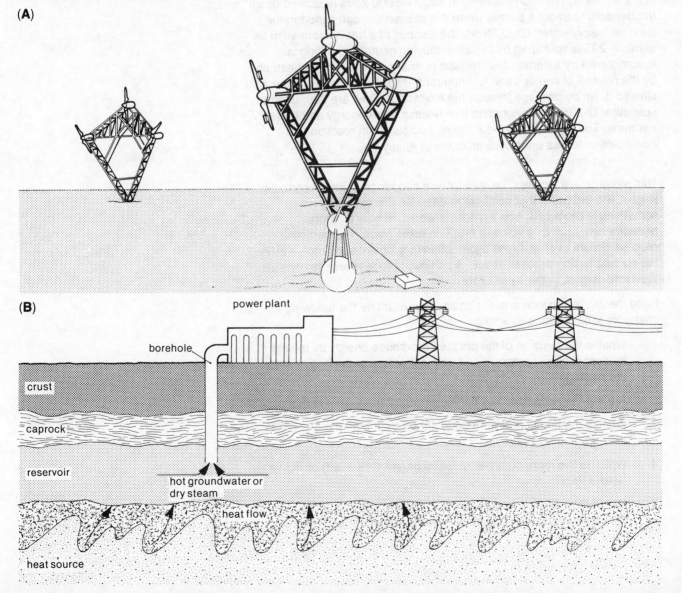

(B)

Writing a Process

1   Read the following:

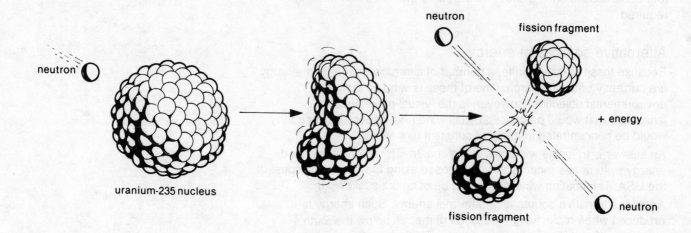

neutron

uranium-235 nucleus

neutron

fission fragment

+ energy

fission fragment

neutron

To produce energy by means of a nuclear fission reactor, the first step is that a fast fission neutron travelling at about 42 000 km/s is slowed down (moderated) to about 1·5 km/s when it is passed through a moderator such as 'heavy water' (D_2O). Next, the nucleus of a heavy atom such as uranium-235 is split apart by this slow-moving neutron. Splitting is accompanied by a tremendous release of energy in the form of heat, and by the release of two or three fast neutrons. These new neutrons are also slowed down by passage through the moderator. They are then used to split other U-235 atoms, which in turn release more energy and more neutrons. The result is a self-sustaining nuclear chain reaction that continually releases enormous amounts of energy.

This passage is a *process*, i.e. it outlines a sequence of inter-connected stages, without gaps, that combine to describe (for example) how something is produced, how a machine works, or how a natural phenomenon such as a volcanic eruption takes place. The particular process occurs over and over again, often in a 'chain' sequence – as in the nuclear fission process above. A particular process always consists of the same stages, in the same order.

Read the *nuclear fission* process again, then examine the following characteristics of process-writing:

1   What is the function of the phrase *To produce energy by means of a nuclear fission reactor...*, and why is it written at the beginning of the passage?

2   Are the stages written in a particular order? If so, what is that order?

3   What is the function of words and phrases such as *the first step, next, then, in turn, the result is...*?

4   Which is the more common: *passive* (is/are VERB + ed) or *active* (VERB + (s))?

5   Identify the passive verbs – are they mostly 'activity' verbs? i.e. do they help you to 'see' the activity taking place?

2 Study and discuss the following diagram. It shows the process of producing electrical power by means of a nuclear fission power plant. Use the diagram to write an account of the process involved. Not all the information in the diagram needs to be included in your writing, i.e. you will need to select items that are essential in describing the process, and disregard what is not essential.

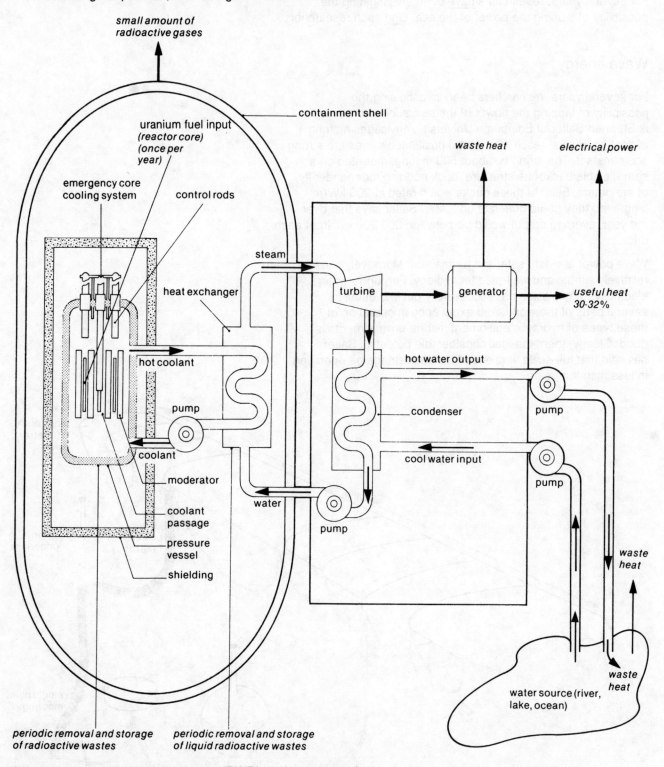

small amount of radioactive gases

containment shell

uranium fuel input (reactor core) (once per year)

emergency core cooling system

control rods

heat exchanger

steam

turbine

generator

waste heat

electrical power

useful heat 30-32%

hot coolant

hot water output

condenser

pump

pump

coolant

pump

moderator

water

cool water input

pump

coolant passage

pressure vessel

shielding

waste heat

waste heat

water source (river, lake, ocean)

periodic removal and storage of radioactive wastes

periodic removal and storage of liquid radioactive wastes

Fig. 6.4 A pressurised water reactor (PWR) nuclear power plant

Grammar Revision

In the following passage ONE word has been omitted from each complete line. Copy the passage, adding the words that you think have been left out, e.g.

For several years, researchers <u>have</u> been investigating the possibility of tapping the power of the sea. <u>One</u> such researcher...

Wave energy

For several years, researchers been investigating the
possibility of tapping the power of the sea. such researcher
is Stephen Salter of Edinburgh University, envisages a string
of floating 'ducks' (each 10 m wide) positioned waves are strong
and constant. The string be about 500 m long, mounted on a
semi-flexible backbone structure, duck nodding independently
of the others. Each of these ducks would rated at 200 kW/m
length, so they could generate up 2 MW. Salter says that over
the year, average output would be between 800 900 kW from each
duck.

Wave power is clean, safe, and permanent. Moreover, uses
relatively simple and well-tried technology. For, underwater
electricity transmission has successfully put into effect in
several parts of the world. And experience in operation of
these types of hydraulic equipment marine environments is
good. Clearly, then, the idea considerable potential. Salter
has said that full-scale versions of his duck strings be operating
in less than ten years.

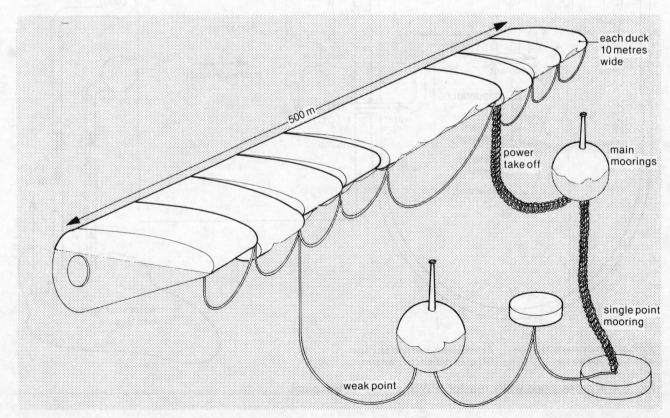

Fig. 6.5 Salter's 'nodding ducks'

Writing Examination Answers

The instruction *outline* (= *indicate*)

A dictionary definition of *outline*: 'to summarise, to show the main features or essential parts'

When the examiner uses the words *outline* or *indicate* he is saying in effect: 'The subject matter of this question is very complicated or lengthy. In 25–30 minutes I do not expect you to go very deeply into it. But I want to see whether you can tell me as many of the major points as you can'. The message is obvious. Do *not* write in detail about only one or two points. Instead, write five or six short paragraphs, each covering one major area of the question. In each paragraph, you should avoid the temptation to go into detail: deal only with the essential subject matter of each area in a concise, simple, direct style of writing. Note also that (unless another part of the question specifically asks you to do so) the question words *outline* or *indicate* do *not* expect you to give your personal opinions, or say whether you agree or disagree, etc. You are simply expected to set out the major facts or components of the subject matter.

Consider the following examination question:

Outline the energy sources currently being developed as alternatives to fossil fuels and nuclear fission.

Identify the components of this question. Then write an answer. A possible answer structure is:

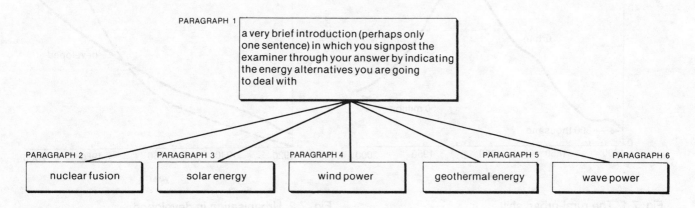

PARAGRAPH 1 — a very brief introduction (perhaps only one sentence) in which you signpost the examiner through your answer by indicating the energy alternatives you are going to deal with

PARAGRAPH 2 — nuclear fusion
PARAGRAPH 3 — solar energy
PARAGRAPH 4 — wind power
PARAGRAPH 5 — geothermal energy
PARAGRAPH 6 — wave power

The paragraph about nuclear fusion might be written in this way:

The largest amount of research into alternative energy sources is being carried out into <u>nuclear fusion.</u> In this process, two nuclei of light atoms (such as deuterium) are joined to form a heavier nucleus (such as helium). A large amount of energy is released in the process. The major advantages of nuclear fusion are: (1) deuterium can be extracted from seawater, therefore it is essentially limitless and cheap; (2) it is much less dangerous than nuclear fission; (3) it could be used for the cheap production of hydrogen gas, a clean fuel which could replace natural gas and petrol.

Comment on:
1 The topic sentence of this paragraph, and the underlining of *nuclear fusion*.
2 The type of information presented, and its order.
3 the numbering and the punctuation of the advantages.

Now complete the writing of the examination answer.

Unit seven: Urbanisation

Study Reading

The life cycle of a city

Already more than 20% of mankind live in urban areas with populations greater than 100 000, and this figure is expected to increase to at least 40% by the year 2000. The rural-urban population shift in the USA (Fig. 7.1) typifies[1] the trend to urbanisation in a developed country. But

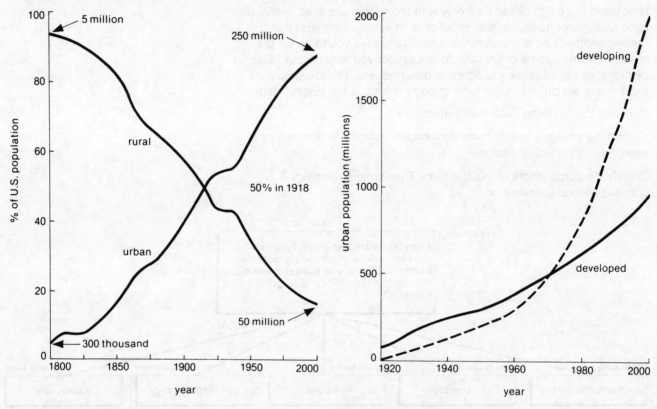

Fig. 7.1 The rural-urban shift in the USA 1800–2000

Fig. 7.2 Urbanisation in developed and developing countries

5 this trend is not limited to developed countries. In developing countries too (Fig. 7.2), where the population is still predominantly rural, rapid urbanisation is occurring. In fact[2], urbanisation in developing countries is taking place more rapidly than that in developed countries. In the former[3], the population of large cities is doubling every 10 to 15 years, and that[4] of
10 many urban slums every 5 to 7 years[5].

These major population shifts within a country or throughout the world – both in developed and developing countries – affect[6] the life cycles of cities. Jay W. Forrester (1969) has developed a crude computer model (Fig. 7.3) for an urban system in an industrialised nation. He analysed a
15 hypothetical[7] city to see how factors such as new and old industry, worker employment, managerial-professional employment and housing interacted[8] over a period of 250 years. Data for each variable[9] were collected, and the projected changes were calculated and plotted with the aid of a computer. The model shows that after a slight lag phase[10] (while

20 initial colonisers[11] are building and slowly expanding the population), there is a dynamic growth phase (the 'J' curve) as industry, housing and employment increase dramatically for a number of years.

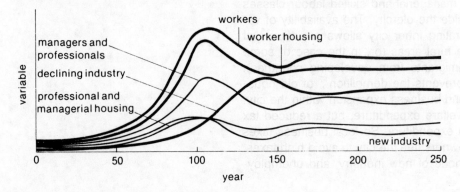

Fig. 7.3 A computer model of the life-cycle of a city

Study reading questions

1 Use your dictionary:
   a) to check the meaning of *typify*.
   b) to complete with the appropriate adjective:
      The rural-urban population shift in the USA is typ.... of the trend to urbanisation in developed countries.

2 What type of information does *in fact* ⦂➻O signpost?
   a) general – specific
   b) cause – effect
   c) statement – restatement in simpler words

3 Which is *the former*?

4 Which word does *that* link back to?

5 What happens to urban slums every 5 to 7 years?

6 *What* affect the life cycles of cities? (Answer in three words.)

7 Use your dictionary to check the meaning and pronunciation of *hypothetical*, and mark the stress. Write down the noun beginning *hypothe...*, and mark its stress.

8 Think of *inter*national and *act*ive. Now say the meaning of *interact*.

9 List some of the variables for which data were collected.

10 By referring to Fig. 7.3, say approximately how long the *slight lag phase* lasted.

11 The word-ending *ers* tells us that *colonisers* are people, and the context that follows tells us what they do. Use this context to guess the meaning of *colonisers*.

Discussion questions

A Verbalise Figs. 7.1, and 7.2. Comment on the data presented, and give your reasons for the changes and projected changes. Relate the data to your own country.

B Find words or phrases that can be replaced by the following:
   taking place, outstripping, movements, examined

The short-term, economically-motivated decisions[12] made in this growth phase often have[13] undesirable long-term effects. The original housing
25 deteriorates[14], and new affluence and the availability of cars and other forms of transportation enable the managerial and skilled labour classes to build a new ring of houses outside the old city. The availability of vacated housing in the now deteriorating inner city allows an influx[15] of unskilled workers, mostly from the rural areas (or, in the case of some
30 developed countries, unskilled immigrants from developing countries). This occupancy[16] by newcomers prevents the demolition[17] of old housing, and further hinders industrial and business expansion within the city. Unemployment rises, generating welfare expenditure, but a reduced tax base[18] from which to finance such expenditure. So local business taxes
35 are raised, and the remaining landowners flee the city to avoid high taxes. This[19] further decreases the likelihood of new industry, and unemployment rises again.

The stage is now set for the second phase of deterioration. The oldest inner city housing eventually deteriorates to the point where it must be
40 demolished. It is usually replaced with housing and office buildings for managerial and professional workers. This provides little employment for the working class, and they move outward into the second ring of housing. Middle and upper classes then develop a new housing ring further from the inner city as stagnation[20] increases.

45 Forrester's preliminary and admittedly crude model shows that the normal practice of raising local taxes may be self-defeating, in that[21] it drives out persons and industries capable of supporting the city. Building expensive motorways and mass transit systems from the suburbs to the inner city can also be counterproductive[22] by making the flight[23] to the suburbs
50 easier. Allowing old housing to stand, or converting it to low-rent housing projects may also be self-defeating in the long run. The migration of additional underemployed persons into a city is controlled[24] by the availability of housing. By removing old housing and refusing to replace it, a city can stop or slow migration of the unskilled, and at the same time provide
55 space for new industries, which can then generate jobs or taxes for the benefit of existing unemployed citizens.

Reference
FORRESTER, Jay W. (1969) *Urban Dynamics.* Cambridge, Mass.: The MIT Press

Study reading questions

[12] *economically-motivated decisions* are:
   a) decisions that are motivated by economic matters.
   b) economic matters that motivate decisions.
   c) motivated decisions that are economic.

[13] *What* often have undesirable long-term effects? (Answer in one word.)

[14] The context suggests that what happens to housing is an *undesirable* long-term effect. Therefore when the original housing *deteriorates*, it . . .

[15] By considering the context, and the prefix *in-*, guess the meaning of *influx*.

[16] *This occupancy* of *what*?

80 [17] What should be done to this old housing?

18 Why is there a reduced tax base (i.e. a smaller income from city taxes)?

19 *What* further decreases the likelihood of new industry?

20 *Stagnation* in the inner city describes the overall economic situation in the second phase of deterioration. Define *stagnation*, then check your definition by using your dictionary.

21 *in that* means approximately the same as:
a) however   b) because   c) therefore

22 When you turn the hands of a clock *counter*-clockwise, you turn them in the opposite direction to their usual movements. What does *counterproductive* mean?

23 the *flight* means:
a) going up   b) flying by airplane   c) running away from difficulty.

24 *What* is controlled by the availability of housing? (Give the extended subject, then its principal noun.)

Discussion questions

C   The text describes three phases in the life of a city, which we may call *growth phase, deterioration phase 1,* and *deterioration phase 2.* Draw the components of each phase as a series of interconnected boxes, viz:

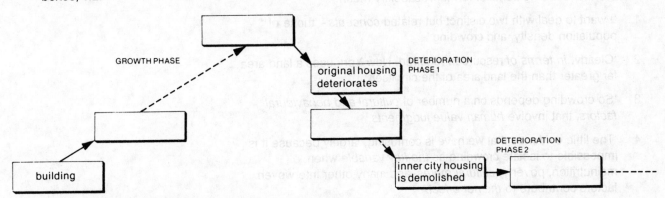

(*You* must decide how many boxes to draw in each phase.)

Now suggest a fourth phase, and draw its component boxes.

D   The final paragraph suggests a number of aspects of the life of a city that may be self-defeating. Extract them from the paragraph, and tabulate them as follows:

SELF-DEFEATING ASPECT	WHY IS IT SELF-DEFEATING?	A BETTER ALTERNATIVE (*you* suggest)
1 The normal practice of raising local taxes		
2		
3		

E   Compare Forrester's model of the life-cycle of a city, with a city you know well. Describe the similarities and differences.

Making Notes from a Talk

You will hear a short talk about some of the effects of urbanisation. A suggested system of headings for your notes is:

1   Population density
1.1   Meaning
1.2   Uneven distribution + examples
1.3   'Effective population density' of New York City
1.4   'Effective population density' of Holland

2   Crowding
2.1   Meaning
2.2   The difficulty of assessing the effects of crowding
2.3   Crowding and poverty
2.4   Crowding and crime
2.5   Crowding and illness
2.6   Crowding and political instability

What did the following items of *formal vocabulary* mean:

1   'I want to deal with two distinct but related *concepts* – those of population density, and crowding.'

2   'Clearly, *in terms of* resources required, New York uses a land area far greater than the land area of the city itself ...'

3   'So crowding depends on a number of *cultural and behavioural factors*, that involve *human value judgments*.'

4   'The little evidence that we have is confusing, largely because it is impossible to isolate crowding as *the key variable* when malnutrition, poverty, *cultural mores*, and many other interwoven factors contribute to *the net effect*.'

5   'There is no doubt that crime is more *prevalent* in large cities.'

6   'Nor has any consistent *correlation* been found between crowding and political instability ...'

Discuss the following points that occurred in the talk:

7   A distinction was drawn between the population density of a city or country, and its 'effective population density' – what is the difference?

8   Why was this distinction stressed?

9   The population density of a city or country can be defined as 'n people per km^2'. Why is it not possible to define crowding in mathematical terms?

10   Is there a correlation between crowding and crime?

11   Is there a correlation between crowding and illness?

Text Completion

Complete the following text by writing suitable sentences that may be added in places (A) and (B). You will probably need to write three or four sentences in each place. The table and graph provide the information required.

Metal poisoning

A large body of research has established that cadmium, mercury and lead are dangerous to human health. The danger is particularly acute in urban areas, because of the concentration of industry and traffic. Cadmium, for example, . . . (A) . . .

Lead has been known to be a poison for many centuries. In fact, there is evidence that it contributed to the fall of the Roman Empire. There is no doubt that in the second century BC, Rome's wealthy ruling class suffered from a disproportionately high level of stillbirths, sterility, and brain damage. And a high lead content has been found in the bones of such ancient Romans. One widely-supported hypothesis is that the cause of both facts was lead poisoning from leaden wine-cups and plates, which only the rich could afford.

In modern times, over 90% of atmospheric lead poisoning comes from car exhausts, as a result of the burning of leaded petrol. Lead poisoning is therefore a particularly serious threat in cities, especially to young children who live near busy city streets. But atmospheric lead pollution is having even a global effect. This has been proved by an analysis of . . . (B) . . .

(A)

METAL	SOURCES	EFFECTS ON HEALTH
cadmium	1. (coal) 2.	e.g. artery
mercury	1. 2.	1. nerve damage 2.
lead	1. 2. (pre-1950s)	1. damage 2.

Fig. 7.4 Sources and effects of metal poisoning

(B)

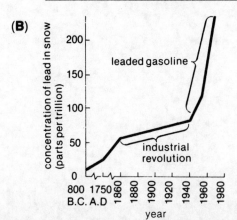

Fig. 7.5 Lead levels in Greenland glaciers

Data Analysis and Comment

Study the following tables, then write a four-paragraph text in which you present and comment on their major contents and implications. Give your writing a suitable heading.

You might like to organise your writing like this:

PARAGRAPH 1: Introduction – a general comment on the effects of urbanisation, + a signpost to your reader indicating the specific effects you are going to write about.

PARAGRAPH 2: Noise – select and analyse important examples, and add relevant comments, e.g. how urban noise can be reduced.

PARAGRAPH 3: Crime – a general comment as to the relationship between urbanisation and crime, then compare the crime rates for different US areas, and suggest reasons for the differences.

PARAGRAPH 4: Inputs and outputs – present the data, then comment on some of the problems that the data represent.

As you write, check that your text reads smoothly, i.e. incorporate inter-sentence and inter-paragraph cohesion.

EXAMPLE	DECIBELS (dbA)	EFFECT AFTER PROLONGED EXPOSURE
jet take-off (close range)	150	eardrum ruptures
steel mill, car horn (1 m)	110	severe pain
jet at 300 m, motor-cycle (8 m), printing plant	100	serious hearing damage
busy urban street, diesel truck	90	hearing damage after 8 hours
average factory, train, noisy office	80	affects concentration and mental health

Fig. 7.6 Common noise levels

AREA	AVERAGE CRIME RATE/ 100 000 PEOPLE/YEAR
cities over 250 000	5 307
cities from 50 000 to 100 000	3 430
suburbs	2 376
rural areas	1 070

Fig. 7.7 The relationship between area and crime rate in the USA

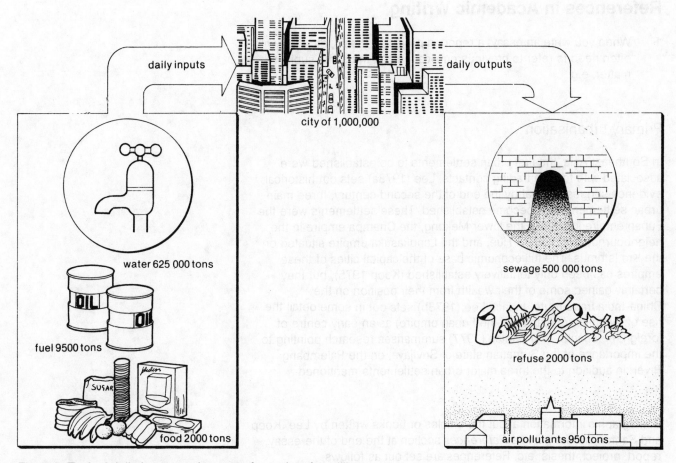

daily inputs

daily outputs

city of 1,000,000

water 625 000 tons

fuel 9500 tons

food 2000 tons

sewage 500 000 tons

refuse 2000 tons

air pollutants 950 tons

Fig. 7.8 Typical daily inputs and outputs for a city of 1 million

Grammar Revision

In the following passage, ONE word has been omitted from each line.
Copy the passage, adding the words that you think have been left out,
e.g.

An increasing number of urban planners <u>are</u> now becoming
aware of the importance <u>of</u> open space.

The importance of open space in urban areas

An increasing number of urban planners now becoming
aware of the importance open space. They realise that towns and
cities areas of open space to make them visually more attractive,
to establish recreational areas, and to absorb noise air pollution.
Furthermore, open space helps to reduce adverse effects of urban
climates, and provides habitats for birds and forms of wildlife
that live in or urban areas.

In the planning stage, open space can be achieved grouping
together domestic accommodation, that areas of land are left open.
Later, when rebuilding, open space can also achieved by buying
old buildings or disused railway tracks, and restoring the land stand
on to a park or playground. The result is that people live in towns
and cities can experience a change the noise and pollution of
traffic, and the 'closed-in' feeling tall buildings.

References in Academic Writing

1 When you write an essay, a report, a project, a thesis, etc., you will often need to refer to previous publications on the same subject matter, e.g.

Primary urbanisation

In Southeast Asia, the first urban settlements to be established were associated with foreign trading contacts. Lee (1978a) sets out historical evidence suggesting that by the end of the second century, three main urban settlements had become established. These settlements were the Funan empire located in the lower Mekong, the Champa empire in the neighbourhood of modern Hué, and the Langkasuka empire situated on the Kra Isthmus. The full economic base of the capital cities of these empires has been only tentatively established (Koop 1975), but they certainly gained some of their wealth from their position on the China-India trade route. In fact, Lee (1978b) sets out in some detail the rise of Vyadhapura (capital of the Funan empire) as an early centre of foreign merchants. And Santos (1977) summarises research pointing to the importance of the Sumatran state of Srivijaya, on the Palembang River, in addition to the three major urban settlements mentioned.

Bibliographic information about the articles or books written by Lee, Koop and Santos are set out in a *References* section at the end of the essay, report, project, thesis, etc. References are set out as follows:

References

KOOP K.L. (1975) Early Trading Centres in Southeast Asia. Bangkok: Thonburi Publishing Company

LEE Mu-Chiao (1978a) The influence of foreign trade routes on primary urbanisation in Southeast Asia. Journal of Demography, 42, 66–78

LEE Mu-Chiao (1978b) The rise of Vyadhapura. In Thomson F.R. and Del Tufo Y.K. (Eds.) A Short History of the Funan Empire. Manila: Palawan

SANTOS T.T. (1977) The origins of Srivijaya as a trading centre. Sumatran Studies, 13, 96–112

The technique of referencing follows very strict conventions. To establish some of the more important conventions, discuss the following:

1 Which criterion decides on the order of the four references in the *References* section?

2 Which criterion decides on the order of the two Lee references?

3 Why are the family names of the authors capitalised?

4 What sort of publication (i.e. article, book, thesis, etc.) are Koop, and Lee (1978b)? What bibliographic information completes these two references?

5 What difference is there between Koop, and Lee (1978b)?

6 What sort of publication are Lee (1978a) and Santos? What bibliographic information completes the references?

7 In all four references, what is underlined?

8 Comment on the punctuation of Koop, and Lee (1978a).

9 Which criterion decides which words begin with a capital letter, and which not?

10 In the text, why is Koop's name in brackets – (Koop 1975)?

2 Read the following extract from a project:

Hong Kong's Mass-Transit Railway

Traffic congestion is a problem that faces all busy cities, and various steps are being taken in cities all over the world to overcome the problem. ... (...) describes the alternatives considered by the Hong Kong Government before the decision was finally taken to build an underground mass-transit railway (MeTRo). A previous research report (..., ...) had projected that in view of Hong Kong's rising population and increasing car ownership, surface transport systems would be unable to cope in the mid-1980s. The financial and sociological implications of the decision to build the MeTRo are fully set out in ... (...). Perhaps the most crucial decision was whether to use the 'cut-and-cover' method, or the 'bored tunnelling' method of constructing the MeTRo. In the event, the latter was considered to be too dangerous in view of the deep foundations of Hong Kong's many high-rise buildings – as argued by ... (...). The 'cut-and-cover' method, with all its disruptions to surface traffic, was therefore adopted.

The following (in random order) are details of the publications you will need to refer to in this project extract:

John Peter *Smithson* wrote a book entitled *Hong Kong's MeTRo: an economic and sociological survey*. The book was published in Singapore by Asian Publishers Ltd., in 1972.

An analysis of the traffic problem facing Hong Kong, and the options available is the title of an article published in 1979 in a journal called *Hong Kong Studies*, pages 73–92. The author is *Chuen* Wing Lam. The article was published in Volume 43.

In 1975, Donald R. *Wilson* and *Yip* Wai Fong edited a book entitled *The principles of constructing high-rise buildings*. Maurice F. *Zaido* contributed an article entitled *Technical aspects of the foundations of Hong Kong's high-rise buildings*. The book was published by Wadsman Publishers, in London.

Hong Kong traffic in the 80s: a problem that must be faced is a Hong Kong Government report published in 1975 by the Hong Kong Government Printer.

You should now:

1 List the author + year of publication for each of the four references, in the order in which they should appear in the project extract, e.g. Johnson (1971).

2 Write the *References* section, following the strict conventions just established.

Writing Examination Answers

The instruction *compare*

A dictionary definition of *compare*: 'to say how one thing is like and unlike another'

Comments: The important point is that *compare* requires you to indicate areas in which the things to be compared are *similar and different*. If you only mention ways in which they are *similar*, or only ways in which they are *different*, then you are only answering half the question. (Note also that *similar* means 'almost the same', *not* 'exactly the same'.)

In answering *compare* questions, choose the most important aspects of the subject matter for comparison. You will probably find it useful to plan your answer:

	THING (X) TO BE COMPARED	THING (Y) TO BE COMPARED
same 1, e.g. same 2, e.g. same 3, e.g.	can be recycled cheap to produce easily available	
different 1, e.g. different 2, e.g. different 3, e.g.	red large heavy	yellow small light

Having spent two or three minutes jotting down ideas in this way, you can then decide on your order of presentation, grouping your ideas into paragraphs by noting paragraph numbers against them.

Consider the following examination question:

Compare the major aspects of urban and rural climates, giving reasons for the comparisons that you make.

Identify the components of this question. Then write an answer, using the data in the following table:

VARIABLE	URBAN LEVELS COMPARED WITH RURAL
Pollutants Particulates Gases (sulphur dioxide, carbon dioxide, carbon monoxide)	10 times more 5 to 25 times more
Cloudiness and fog Cloud cover Winter fog Summer fog	5 to 10 per cent more 100 per cent more 30 per cent more
Precipitation Rain Snow	5 to 10 per cent more 5 to 15 per cent less
Relative humidity Winter Summer	2 per cent less 8 per cent less

Solar radiation	15 to 20 per cent less
Temperature Annual mean Winter average	0·5 to 1·0°C higher 1 to 2°C higher
Visibility	5 to 30 per cent less
Wind speed Annual mean Calms (stagnant air)	20 to 30 per cent less 5 to 20 per cent more

The following are the major factors that account for this data:

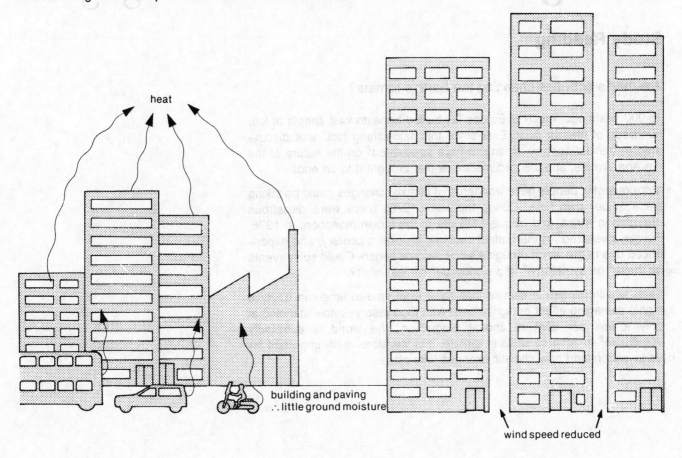

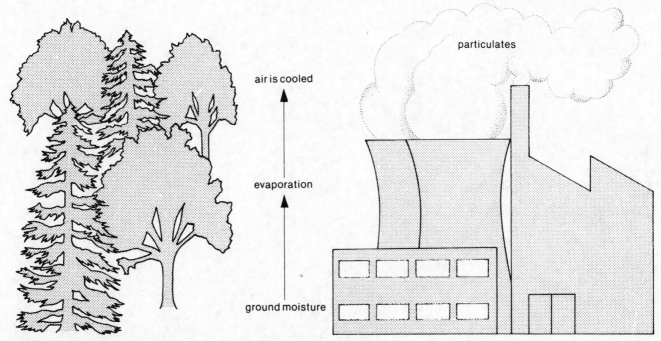

No answer structure is provided this time. Instead, when you have planned your answer, you should group your ideas into paragraphs by noting paragraph numbers against them, then decide on your paragraph order.

Remember that in a *compare* answer, *you must include points of similarity*, as well as points of difference.

Unit eight: Is the Earth's climate changing?

Study Reading

Are man's activities changing the Earth's climate?

18 000 years ago, much of Europe lay buried beneath vast sheets of ice, hundreds of metres thick. Ever since this astonishing fact[1] was discovered in the last century, scientists have speculated[2] on the nature of the Ice Age climate, and the circumstances that brought it to an end.

5 More recently, people have wondered[2] if climatic changes could be taking place in our own time. During the early 1970s there were disastrous droughts in Africa, and frequent failures of the Indian monsoon. In 1976, Europe sweltered[3] in the hottest summer for over a century, and experienced one of the worst droughts since records began. Could such events
10 as these[4] be symptoms[5] of a worldwide[6] climatic shift?

Even small changes in climate that occur from time to time can have[7] a highly damaging effect on agriculture. With food reserves now standing at only a few per cent of annual production, the world is extremely vulnerable[8] to adverse shifts in climate. It is therefore vitally important for
15 us to understand how climatic changes take place.

Study reading questions

1 *Which* fact is astonishing? *Why* is it astonishing?

2 '...scientists have *speculated*...' and '...people have *wondered*...'
Speculate on the slight difference in meaning between these two words.

3 Use the context to work out the meaning of *sweltered*.

4 *Which*?

5 The events of the early 1970s and of 1976 are described as possible
symptoms of a worldwide climatic shift. Examine the context, then explain
in a few words the meaning of *symptoms*. (Think also of the *symptoms* of
a disease or illness.)

6 By examining the word parts *world* and *wide*, express in a few words the
meaning of *worldwide*.

7 *What* can have a highly damaging effect on agriculture? (Answer in three
words, then one.)

8 *Adverse* means unfavourable or hostile. *Vulnerable* therefore means 'able
to be...'

Discussion questions

A   We are told that scientists last century discovered that there was an
    Ice Age in Europe 18 000 years ago, but we are not told *how* they
    came to this conclusion. Can you suggest how they did so?

B   What do you think were the immediate and medium-term
    consequences of the climatic events in Africa and India in the early
    1970s?

C   Find words or phrases that can be replaced by the following:
    terminated it
    occurring
    statistics were maintained
    very serious
    stocks

Equally important is the need to understand *why* such changes occur.
Until recently we have assumed that variations in regional and global climate observed over the centuries resulted from natural phenomena. But
there is now some tentative evidence suggesting that man's activities
20 are already affecting local climates, and may affect regional and even
global climatic patterns in the future.

There are several ways in which man could be altering regional and
global climate. First, the carbon dioxide content of the atmosphere is increasing, as a result of burning fossil fuels. Second, the atmospheric
25 transparency is decreasing, because of particulate matter (dust, sul-
phates, liquid droplets, etc.) being injected into the atmosphere from
such activities as industry, cars and agriculture. Next – deforestation[9/10],
irrigation[10], urbanisation[10] and agriculture are changing the albedo
of the Earth's surface. (The albedo is the percentage of incoming solar
30 radiation that is directly reflected outward.) Fourth, the atmosphere is
being directly heated by the burning of fossil and nuclear fuels. And
finally, oil films from spills and blowouts[11] are altering the rate of thermal
energy transfer[12] between the oceans and the atmosphere.

Discussion questions

D   The following are possible topics of the five paragraphs of this
passage, with each set of three possibilities in random order.
Number the sets in an order that follows the organisation of the
passage, then from each set select a), b) or c) that best
expresses the topic of each paragraph.

PARAGRAPH

?	a)	the effect of climatic changes on food supply
	b)	the importance of understanding how changes in climate occur
	c)	the effect of small climatic changes

?	a)	the reasons for the Ice Age climate
	b)	Europe's climate 18 000 years ago
	c)	scientists' speculation on the Ice Age climate

4	a)	the importance of understanding why changes in climate occur
	b)	climatic changes resulting from natural phenomena
	c)	climatic changes resulting from man's activities

?	a)	climatic changes resulting from man's activities
	b)	the effects of atmospheric changes on global climate
	c)	climatic changes caused by industrialisation

?	a)	climatic changes in the 1970s
	b)	the effects of climatic changes in the 1970s
	c)	the possibility of global climatic changes taking place in our own time

Read the five topics you have chosen, one after the other. They should
interconnect in meaning. *Do* they?

Study reading questions

9 Think of *deduct* and *detach*. What is the meaning of *deforestation*?

10 Use your dictionary to complete the following:

NOUN	irrigation	urbanisation	deforestation
VERB			
ADJECTIVE	—		—

(Mark the stress in each case, and notice where it changes.)

11 The context is oil and oceans. With this context in mind, work out the meaning of *blowouts*, by examining its word parts. Say where (in this example) a *blowout* takes place.

12 *Thermal energy transfer* is:
a) the heat of energy that is transferred.
b) the heat produced by the transfer of energy.
c) the transfer of energy in the form of heat.

Discussion questions

E Using the items in the final paragraph, copy and complete the following table:

	MAN'S ACTIVITY →	IMMEDIATE RESULT →	POSSIBLE LONGER-TERM CONSEQUENCES (*you* suggest)
1	burning fossil fuels		increased air temperature near Earth → melting of polar ice caps → flooding of cities and agricultural land at present sea-level
2		decrease of the atmospheric transparency	
3			
4			
5			

Grammar Revision

In the following passage, ONE word has been omitted from each line.
Copy the passage, adding the words that you think have been left out, e.g.

One probable cause of short-term climatic change <u>is</u> volcanic activity.

Volcanic activity and climatic change

One probable cause of short-term climatic change volcanic activity.
Violent volcanic outbursts shoot vast clouds dust and gases
high the upper atmosphere. Once there, the sulphur-containing
gases react form tiny droplets of sulphuric acid. Together with
minute silicate dust particles, they dispersed by the upper winds
all over the Earth. Such volcanic particles the upper atmosphere
often remain suspended years. They therefore cool the Earth by
reducing the intensity of sunlight can reach the surface. For
example, the volcano Tambora (in Indonesia) erupted in 1815,
it was of the greatest volcanic explosions in centuries. It was
surely a coincidence that the summer of 1816 in Europe and
North America was one of the coldest and wettest record.

Making Notes from a Talk

You will hear a short talk about one of the ways in which man's activities might be altering the climate. A suggested system of headings for your notes is:

(main heading)

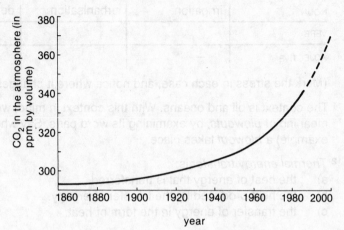

1 CO_2 in the atmosphere
1.1   Increased concentration (+ graph)
1.2   Reasons
1.3   The function of atmospheric CO_2
      (+ diagram)
1.4   The effect of increased CO_2 content
      on average air temperature

2   The effect of increased air temperature
2.1   The Antarctic ice cap
2.2   The Arctic ice cap

3   The hypothesis v. the facts

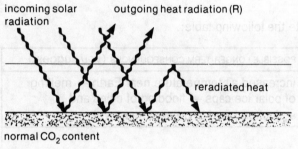

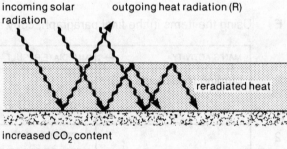

You heard the following *colloquial expressions* in the talk. What did they mean?

1   'You're possibly thinking – so what? How does an increased concentration of CO_2 in the atmosphere influence the Earth's temperature?' (What is a more formal way of saying *so what?*?)

2   '...this is where we run across the "Greenhouse Effect".' (Try to visualise yourself *running across* something – what happens?)

3   'A 1 to 2°C change would significantly modify global climate. It could trigger the relatively rapid melting of the floating Arctic ice pack.' (When *X triggers Y*, what sort of thing happens? – think of the trigger of a gun.)

4   'This fall since 1945 certainly doesn't tie in with the "greenhouse" model.' (Consider the context, then suggest what happens when *X does not tie in with Y*.)

What did the following items of *formal vocabulary* mean?

5   'Assuming that energy is arriving from the sun at a *constant* rate, then as the level of CO_2 increases, the average surface temperature of the Earth should rise.'

6   'This possible effect of CO_2 on the Earth's climate was first *mooted* in 1863...'

7   'This is the *hypothesis*, then. But what's actually happening?'

Data Analysis and Comment

Study and discuss the following graphs. Then use them as the basis for writing a three-paragraph text entitled *The effects of global temperature change on grain reserves.*

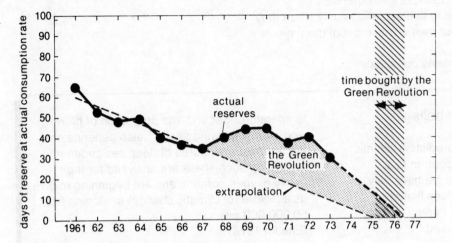

Fig. 8.1 The decline in world food grain reserves

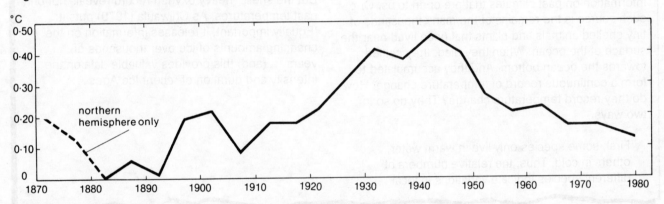

Fig. 8.2 The variation of global mean surface temperatures since 1870

The following is a possible text structure:

PARAGRAPH 1: the decline in world food grain reserves, especially:
 – the causes
 – the effect of the Green Revolution on reserves
 – can we expect further technological advances to improve yield?
 – can we use more chemical fertilizer to increase yield?

PARAGRAPH 2: the variation of global mean surface temperatures, especially the present trend

PARAGRAPH 3: the consequences on world food grain reserves of a global decline in mean surface temperatures, especially:
 – lower yield?
 – shorter growing seasons?
 – increased/decreased crop resistance to pests and disease?
 – is there anything that can be done?

Add other comments that you consider relevant. Check your paragraph structure – especially your topic sentences, and inter-sentence and inter-paragraph cohesion.

Quotations in Academic Writing

1   When writing an essay, a report, a project, a thesis, etc., it is sometimes useful to quote an extract from someone else's writing – perhaps in order to quote the opinion of an authority on the subject matter, or to cite the source of facts that might otherwise be disputed. However, it is advisable to use quotations only when they serve a specific purpose; use your own words most of the time.

The following extract from a report contains quotations:

Past climatic information from shells

One of the most valuable means of predicting climatic change is to explore climates of the past. In fact, Fernande (1970) claims that '... once we have fully pieced together the millions of tiny clues that still remain of past climates, our ability to control the future of mankind will be significantly increased.'

We have only recently begun to realise the sources of information on past climates that are open to us. One such source is the remains of the many thousands of tiny shelled animals and plants that once lived near the surface of the ocean. When they died, they settled towards the ocean bottom. And they accumulated to form a continuous record of temperature change. How do they record temperature change? They do so in two ways.

First, some species only live in warm water, others in cold. Thus, the relative numbers of different species indicate variations in local temperature. Second, the proportion of heavy oxygen in a growing shell ... also depends on the temperature. Cores of deep sea sediment containing such shells are analysed for their heavy oxygen content, and are beginning to give us a picture (of climatic change) stretching back 50 000 000 years.
(Ettetim 1978)

But the shells' heavy oxygen record reveals not only past temperatures. As Chiwaula (1979) puts it: 'Equally important, it releases information on the changing amounts of ice over thousands of years ... (and) this provides valuable data on the intensity and duration of recent Ice Ages ...'

As with referencing, there are various conventions associated with quotations. To establish the most important ones, consider the following:

1   The three dots (...) are called *an ellipsis mark*. In the Fernande quotation:
    a)   What does the ellipsis mark signify?
    b)   Comment on the punctuation at the beginning and end of the quotation.

2   In the Ettetim quotation:
    a)   Why is it not set out in the same way as the Fernande quotation? i.e. Why is it not set out in the body of the text, within quotation marks?
    b)   How do we know that it is, in fact, a quotation?
    c)   How *is* it set out?
    d)   What does the ellipsis mark between *shell* and *also* signify?
    e)   Why do the words *of climatic change* appear inside brackets?

3   In the Chiwaula quotation:
    a)   Where have words or sentences been omitted?
    b)   Why does the word *and* appear inside brackets?
    c)   Comment on the punctuation at the beginning and end of the quotation.

2 In the following extract from a project, quotations are to be inserted in places (A), (B), and (C). (The quotations are in random order after the text.)

Tree growth and climate

As a tree grows, a cylindrical layer is laid down each growing season on the inside of the bark. The layer is manufactured by photosynthesis from CO_2 and rainwater. A very small proportion of the oxygen and hydrogen atoms in rainwater are heavier than normal; and the exact proportion is determined by the temperature during the growing season. Each growth ring preserves this isotopic proportion. Scientists can therefore extract a thin core from the tree, and measure the isotopic proportion by means of a mass spectrometer. Consequently, (A) But most living trees will only provide climate records going back a few hundred years

Fortunately, (B)

However, 5 500 years is still only about one-millionth of the age of the Earth. Another aspect of tree records enables us to go much further back. This is the fact that every species of growing tree sheds its own distinctive pollen grains annually, and these tiny grains accumulate in lakes. Different species of tree thrive in different climatic conditions. Therefore (C). For example, Carbon-14 dating of European pollen sequences reveals climatic change since the last Ice Age.

Quotations
* Pollen records enable researchers to compile climatic records stretching back over thousands of years, since the relative proportions found in lake deposits indicate the proportions of different species growing at a particular period. And this in turn reflects climatic change over thousands of years, as in the case of certain European climatic records established by pollen sequences.

(An extract from an article in a journal entitled *Climatology*. It was written in 1980 by *I.M. Selikoff*, and is called *Pollen records: a clue to past climates*. The article was published as pages 12–19, volume 40.)

* Each tree can be analysed by means of mass spectography, and can therefore 'remember' the changes in climate that have taken place during its life.

(An extract from *Climatic records of the past*, page 127, published by Mexico Publishing Co., Mexico City, 1975. The book was edited by *S.T. Ramiro*, and the extract is from an article in the book written by *P.R. Sanchos*, entitled *Mass spectography as an instrument for measuring climatic change.*)

* One of the drawbacks of establishing climatic changes by 'tree-ring' analysis is the relatively short life of a tree. But there is additional information close at hand: the climatic data locked inside living trees can be cross-matched with that in nearby dead trees, i.e. building timber or tree stumps. This is a painstaking, time-consuming process, requiring very careful, specialist analysis. But in this way, we can sometimes build up climatic records stretching back 5 500 years. Wood isotope studies are still in their infancy, but are likely to prove particularly valuable in countries where tree growth is extremely sensitive to climatic change.

(An extract from a UNESCO report, published in New York, 1972, page 569, by the United Nations Organisation. The report is entitled *Climate and Food.*)

You should now:

a) Decide on the correct order in which appropriate parts of the three extracts should be inserted in the text as quotations.

b) Decide which *parts* of the extracts should be included as quotations, paying particular attention to the information in the text before and after the quotation.

c) Rewrite the text, including the three quotations, paying particular attention to ellipsis marks, punctuation at the beginning and end of each quotation, and referencing (e.g. (Johnson 1971)).

d) Write the *References* section, following the conventions established on pp. 86 and 87

Text Completion

Complete the following text by writing suitable sentences that may be
added in places (A) and (B). You will probably need to write three or four
sentences in each place. The diagrams provide the information required.

Temperature inversion

Air does not stay in the same place very long. This is because currents of
air circle the Earth, carrying away pollutants that they meet. As a result,
even the dirtiest industrial cities have their air changed and cleaned. In
addition to air currents, upward movements of air also help to remove
pollutants from the Earth's atmosphere. . . . (A) . . .

But sometimes these upward movements of air do not take place. This
phenomenon is known as temperature inversion. . . . (B) . . . Whatever the
combination of reasons, a temperature inversion traps the air pollutants of
an industrial city, and they become more and more concentrated and
form what is known as *smog*. This is air that is heavy with dust, smoke,
hydrocarbons and other pollutants. Smog is a very serious threat to the
health of people living in industrial cities.

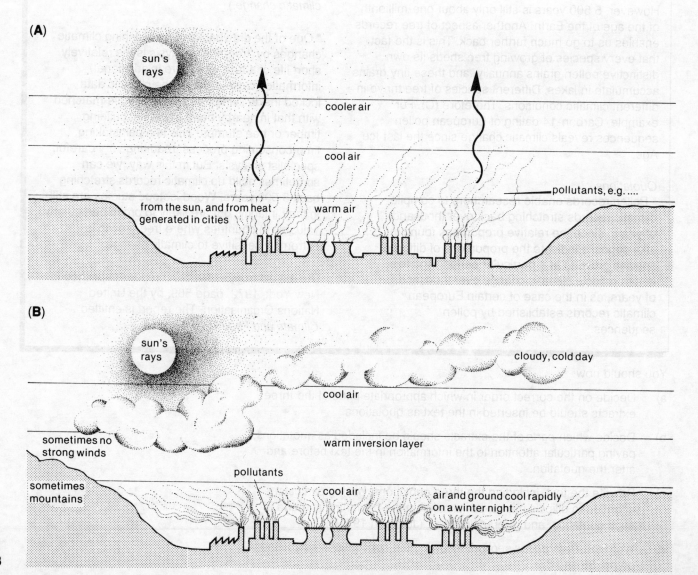

Writing Examination Answers

The instruction *write notes* (= *prepare notes, set out notes*)

A dictionary definition of *notes*: 'a brief written record of facts to aid the memory, probably to be expanded on a subsequent occasion'

Notes questions are essentially factual, and are much more 'right or wrong' than most other types of question. They usually concern a lengthy, complex subject matter, which the examiner realises you cannot cover completely in examination essay-type form. He therefore asks you to give your answer in note form. It is clear, therefore, that the examiner expects a considerable number of facts, so only tackle a *notes* question if you know a considerable amount about the subject matter.

Notes mean different things to different people. The important thing is — what does the examiner mean? The following would be very acceptable to an examiner as part of a *notes* answer:

---

3 Depletion of ozone layer

3.1 Ozone layer protects Earth from harmful ultraviolet radiation.

3.2 Increased skin cancer if ultraviolet radiation increased.

3.3 Depletion of ozone layer possible as result of nitrogen oxide emissions from supersonic transport planes (SSTs), and gradual buildup of freon from aerosol spray cans.

3.4 In USA, concern over depletion of ozone layer from SSTs led to abandonment of SST programme.

From this example, you will see that:

— There is an underlined section heading.
— Each point under the section heading is identified by letter or number. (The decimal system is preferable, but there are other methods.)
— The presentation of points in a logical order is important.
— The emphasis is on setting down 'point-scoring' facts, rather than essay-style presentation.
— Sentences are much shorter than usual.
— Articles (*a, an, the*) are omitted.
— There are no contractions (such as *won't* or *they'll*).

Consider the following examination question:

You have been asked to give a talk to a class of college students on the subject: 'Ways in which man is changing the Earth's climate, and the possible effects of such changes'. PREPARE NOTES for your talk.

Identify the components of this question, then write an answer. You may wish to include:

1 CO_2 buildup and Greenhouse Effect
2 Particle pollution
3 Depletion of ozone layer (Include the example above, and expand it if you wish.)
4 Direct heating of atmosphere (See also pp. 66, 88 and 89.)
5 Changing albedo

(Information on these points is contained in various sections of this unit.)

Appendix A

Using your Dictionary

1 Introduction

1.1 Which dictionary?

For advanced study in English you need an appropriate dictionary. You are recommended to buy the *Longman Dictionary of Contemporary English* (LDOCE).

1.2 Alphabetical order

Words in a dictionary appear in alphabetical order, i.e. according to the order of the letters of the alphabet. The following words are in alphabetical order:

coronary
coroner
emulsion
enamel
encipher
encircle
negligible
negotiate
negotiation

You will see that *coroner* comes before *emulsion*, because *c* comes before *e* in the alphabet. But why does *enamel* come before *encipher*? The first two letters (*en*) of each word are the same. Therefore the third letter determines the order in which the two words appear in the dictionary. The *a* of *enamel* comes before the *c* of *encipher* in the alphabet, and so *enamel* comes before *encipher*.

In the same way, put the following words in alphabetical order:

scrape	asbestos	scrawl	marvellous
finger	scrupulous	obviate	answer
resident	marsupial	amplify	crampon
obtuse	malnutrition	cynic	marvel
ambition	scrap	monochrome	obverse

2 Using your dictionary to find the meaning of a word

The best way to learn new words and their meanings is by *reading*. By constantly meeting a word in its context, you will gradually acquire a group of ideas about the word's overall meaning. This is a much better way of learning the meaning of words than by referring to your dictionary each time you feel unsure, and by getting from it a rather narrow definition (which you will probably quickly forget).

But sometimes you will *have* to use your dictionary, when you get no help from the context in understanding the meaning of an unfamiliar word. When you do so, remember three things:

2.1 Often, the lexicographer (dictionary-writer) will provide a sentence –
in italics – containing the word in context. This sentence will
probably tell you as much about the meaning of the word as the
definition itself. For example:

(dissipate) *He tried to dissipate the smoke by opening a window.*

2.2 Many words of the same spelling have two or more different
meanings. For example, *fret* can mean:

to be worried or bad-tempered about small things;

or to wear something away by continual rubbing or biting;

or to make patterns on wood by cutting or sawing it;

or one of the metal ridges on the fingerboard of a guitar, which
guide the fingers.

In such a case, bear in mind the context in which the unfamiliar
word occurs, and read the various possibilities of that spelling until
you find the definition that fits the context. For example, which *fret* is
contained in the following sentence?

*The water came from a channel fretted down the hillside by means
of a stream.*

2.3 There will be some words, particularly specialist technical words,
that you will not find in a general dictionary such as LDOCE. In that
case, you will need to refer to (for example) *An Elementary
Scientific and Technical Dictionary* (Flood and West), *Longman
Dictionary of Scientific Usage* (Godman and Payne), or a specialist
dictionary for your particular subject-matter.

Use your dictionary to find the meanings (in their contexts) of the
italicised words in the following sentences. Write a brief definition of each
italicised word.

To help with examination revision, the intelligent student often uses
mnemonics.

To make them easier to identify, some coins have *milled* edges.

I *deferred* to my father's opinion about my career, since he is wiser and
more experienced.

Shale oil is being produced in larger quantities in the USA since the fuel
crisis.

When I realised my doctor could not cure me, I decided to go to a
chiropractor.

Unless you *size* paper, it will be too porous to write on.

Being a *mortician* is a profession in which you meet lots of people.

3 Spelling

At first sight, it might seem that using your dictionary to find the spelling of a word is impossible. Perhaps you are thinking: 'How can I find a word when I do not know the letters it contains?' But your task is certainly not impossible, because with a little intelligent thought *you can usually work out what letters the sounds can represent*.

Suppose your lecturer has used a word that sounded like 'mulibdinim', and the word was used several times in a lecture about the production of different metals. This context is important, in order for you to be sure that you have, in fact, found the word you were looking for. Suppose you found in your dictionary the word *mulidinerm* – 'a spiky plant found in Central America'. This has clearly nothing to do with metals, and so is not the word you are looking for. The first thing, then, is to keep in mind the *context* in which you heard the word.

For purposes of checking spelling, the first three or four letters of the word are the most important. So the question you must ask yourself is: 'How might these first few letters be spelt?' We know the word begins with *m*, then a vowel sound, then *l* (possibly *ll*). How might the vowel sound be spelt? 'mul' might be spelt *mul-*, *mil-*, *mol-*, *mel-*, or *mal-*, and there are likely to be still more possibilities. We now take each of these spelling possibilities, starting with the more likely ones, looking for a word which probably continues with the letters *?bd?n?m*, and has something to do with metals. By using this method, we will find the word we are looking for under mol... – *molybdenum*: 'a silver-white metal that is a simple substance used especially in strengthening and hardening steel'.

What have we done to find the spelling of this new word?

1   First, we have kept in mind the context in which we heard the word, in order to be sure that we have, in fact, found the *correct* word, and not one that sounds the same but is spelt differently.

2   We have then asked ourselves how the first three or four letters might be spelt.

3   Starting with the most likely of the alternatives, we have then taken each of the spelling possibilities, bearing in mind the context (metals), and the following sounds, especially consonants (*?bd?n?m*), until the correct word was found in the dictionary.

Now *you* try. Imagine you have heard the following words in a lecture, and you want to find out how they are spelt. Use your dictionary to find the spelling of each word.

CONTEXT	WORD SOUNDS LIKE	SPELLING
transport	'telfa'	?
rocks	'poorfiree'	?
weather	'mailstrum'	?
general	'kunundrim'	?
medicine	'bassillis'	?
geography	'maridyinal'	?
general	'vakyuous'	?
airplanes	'nassell'	?

4 Pronunciation

4.1 The sounds of English

Each entry in a dictionary includes a *transcription* of the pronunciation. This consists of a string of symbols immediately following the headword[1] e.g. /ɪkstɪŋgwɪʃ/[2].

You know most of the symbols in /ɪkstɪŋgwɪʃ/, with the exception of /ɪ/, /ŋ/ and /ʃ/. (All the symbols are based on an internationally-agreed set – the 'International Phonetic Alphabet' – which can be used to represent the sounds of any language). A key to the symbols is given at the front of the dictionary; the examples given for each symbol should help you to interpret the sounds they represent. (How are /ŋ/ and /ʃ/ pronounced?)

The great value of the transcription of a word is that it tells you *clearly* how the word is normally pronounced – you may need to refer to the key from time to time, but less and less often as you become familiar with the symbols.

Use the key at the front of your dictionary to write the ordinary spelling of:

smɔːl tʃeɪndʒɪz ɪn klaɪmɪt kən hæv ə sɪərɪəs ɪfekt ɒn

ægrɪkʌltʃə. ɪt ɪz ðeəfɔː ɪmpɔːtənt tuː ʌndəstænd haʊ ənd waɪ

klaɪmætɪk tʃeɪndʒɪz teɪk pleɪs.

4.2 Stress

A word in English can be divided into *syllables* when spoken. For example, the word *man* contains one syllable, the word *finger* contains two syllables (fing-ger), *telephone* has three (te-le-phone), and *scientific* has four (sci-en-ti-fic).

Say the following words slowly, and decide how many syllables they each contain:

transmit	viscous
assemble	circulate
regulation	environmental
consequently	hence
respectively	distribution

Some words in English are *mono*syllabic (i.e. contain only one syllable: *mono* = one). Examples are *some, way, men, kicked*. Some words are *poly*syllabic (i.e. contain more than one syllable: *poly* = many). Examples are *classify, contain, experiment, centrifugal*.

---

1) The *headword* is the principal word of a 'family' of words, from which *derivatives* are formed. For example, *geology* is the headword and *geological* is its derivative.

2) Slant lines // are used to enclose transcriptions in phonetic symbols.

Polysyllabic words *always* contain one (and only one) syllable which stands out from the other syllables. For example, we say eduCAtion, STUdent, eQUIPment, TECHnical. In these words, the syllables that are capitalised and underlined are spoken with more force than the other syllables. The syllable that stands out in this way is said to be *stressed*. It receives the *stress*.

Mark the stressed syllable in each of the following words by putting a stress mark before it – the first one is marked for you.

e'quipment	malleable	installation	potential
quadrilateral	procedure	property	nuclear
compromise	detonator	development	invisible
function	systematic	eliminate	perimeter
irrelevant	immerse	considerable	fumigate

4.3 The marking of stress in dictionaries

Different dictionaries indicate stress in different ways. In LDOCE, for example, stress is shown by a small mark /'/ immediately before the stressed syllable, e.g. *scientific* is marked /saɪən'tɪfɪk/. Most dictionaries show primary (main) and secondary (less forceful) stress. However, you are advised to ignore the secondary stress marks. If you can pronounce a word with *primary* stress on the correct syllable, then this is all that matters.

The following words have primary stress marked. How are they pronounced?

dimension	/daɪ'menʃən/
negligible	/'neglɪdʒəbəl/
advertisement	/əd'vɜːtɪsmənt/
inculcate	/'ɪnkʌlkeɪt/
reverberate	/rɪ'vɜːbəreɪt/
prestige	/pre'stiːʒ/

The following 'nonsense' words have primary stress marked. How are they pronounced?

/rə'mɪsɪn/	/pɪ'pɪpɪŋ/
/'prɪ mət/	/pɪpɪ'pɪŋ/
/'θɔɪkətə/	/hærɪ'lɪnɪni/
/θɔ'kɔɪtə/	/sɪ'bəʊrə/
/tʃɪpə'reəri/	/bɪ'kɒnɪkɪz/
/hɑː'fweɪ/	/ðɪ'jend/

Appendix B

Using the Library

1   Classification systems

To get the most out of your studies, it is essential to know how to use the library to find information. In fact, as soon as you begin your course in your place of study, you are strongly advised to spend some time in the library, to acquaint yourself with the library's procedures and systems.

The most important system to understand is the library's *classification system*. All books in a library are classified (arranged into classes or divisions) so that a reader can easily find a particular book. Different libraries have different Classification Systems, but whichever system a library uses, each subject has a *classification* (or *class*) number. This number is the 'key' to finding the book you want.

2   The subject index

To find out what books the Library has on a subject, the first step is to refer to the *alphabetical subject index*. This is arranged alphabetically according to subject. In some libraries, the Subject Index consists of a computer-produced list in book form; in other libraries, it consists of a set of cards. But the information in the Subject Index is always the same, i.e. it gives a *class number* for each subject, e.g.

SUBJECT	CLASS NUMBER*
Computer programming	001.642
Geology	550
Insurance	368
Mechanical Drawing	604.2

When using the Subject Index, always look under the most specific heading. For example, Shipbuilding is such a large subject that you would have to be more specific and decide what *aspect* of Shipbuilding you were interested in. If you wanted to find the Class Number of 'ways in which copper is used in shipbuilding', then look under:

Copper: materials: engineering: shipbuilding   623.820 722

On the other hand, if you were interested in 'statistics about population growth', then look under:

Statistics: Populations 312

The *subject index*, then, will give you the *class number* of the subject concerned.

3   Catalogues

When you have found the Class Number of the subject concerned, your next step is to find out what books the library has on that subject. To do so, you must consult the *catalogues*. Catalogues list all the books in the library.

In most libraries, the Catalogue is divided into two sections: the *subject* (or *classified*) *catalogue*, and the *author/title* (or *name and title*) *catalogue*.

---

*   Class Numbers used in the examples in this Appendix are part of the Dewey Decimal Classification system.

105

3.1 Subject Catalogue

This is arranged alphabetically according to subject. Consult the Subject Catalogue when you do not have a specific author or title, but when you want to find out what books the library has on the subject concerned, e.g.

(Subject Heading: *Climatology*)

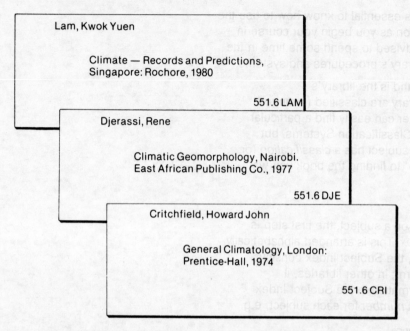

Lam, Kwok Yuen

Climate — Records and Predictions,
Singapore: Rochore, 1980

551.6 LAM

Djerassi, Rene

Climatic Geomorphology, Nairobi.
East African Publishing Co., 1977

551.6 DJE

Critchfield, Howard John

General Climatology, London:
Prentice-Hall, 1974

551.6 CRI

As with the Subject Index, use the most specific heading you can, when looking up a subject in the Subject Catalogue.

3.2 Author/Title Catalogue

If you know the author's name (e.g. Peter G. SMITH) and/or the title of the book you want (e.g. *Pollution Control in the Plastics and Rubber Industry*), consult the *author/title catalogue*. This is arranged alphabetically, according to a combination of the author's family name and the title of the book, e.g.

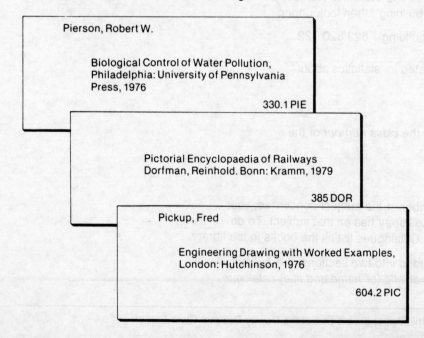

Pierson, Robert W.

Biological Control of Water Pollution,
Philadelphia: University of Pennsylvania
Press, 1976

330.1 PIE

Pictorial Encyclopaedia of Railways
Dorfman, Reinhold. Bonn: Kramm, 1979

385 DOR

Pickup, Fred

Engineering Drawing with Worked Examples,
London: Hutchinson, 1976

604.2 PIC

3.3 How to read a catalogue entry

Each catalogue entry is a complete bibliographic description of the book concerned, e.g.

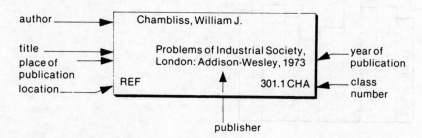

author ──→
title ──→
place of publication ──→
location ──→

Chambliss, William J.

Problems of Industrial Society,
London: Addison-Wesley, 1973

REF   301.1 CHA

←── year of publication
←── class number

publisher

3.4 Arrangement of books on the shelves

To find a book on the shelves, you should copy down the location, author, title and class number from the catalogue entry. The *class number* is the most important item, as it tells you exactly where the book is shelved. Under most classification systems, books are shelved numer-alphabetically. This means that they are shelved first according to their class number, and books with the same class number are shelved according to the first three letters of the author's family name:

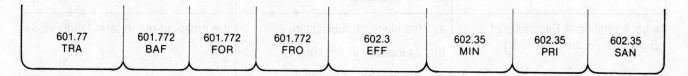

| 601.77 TRA | 601.772 BAF | 601.772 FOR | 601.772 FRO | 602.3 EFF | 602.35 MIN | 602.35 PRI | 602.35 SAN |

4 Classroom exercises

4.1 Study the following catalogue entries, then complete the table below.

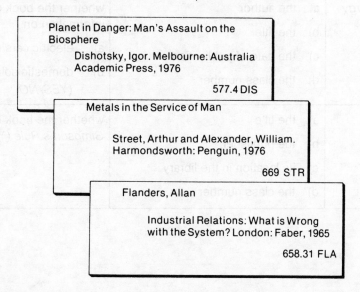

Planet in Danger: Man's Assault on the Biosphere

Dishotsky, Igor. Melbourne: Australia Academic Press, 1976

577.4 DIS

Metals in the Service of Man

Street, Arthur and Alexander, William. Harmondsworth: Penguin, 1976

669 STR

Flanders, Allan

Industrial Relations: What is Wrong with the System? London: Faber, 1965

658.31 FLA

CLASS NUMBER	TITLE	AUTHOR	YEAR OF PUBLICATION

4.2 In which order should books with the following class numbers be shelved? (The first one is done for you).

821.74	ROB
821.814	FIN
821.74	BAB
821.7	SUT
820.9143	ANT
822.076	HIL
821.74	SUT
822.32	TUT
822.076	MIN

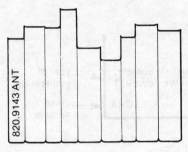

5 Practical work in the library

Complete at least six of the following:

YOU NEED TO KNOW IF THE LIBRARY HAS...	FIND OUT (from the catalogue)...	FIND OUT (from the book itself)...
a book written by Bruce *Cooper*, about *writing reports*	a) the title of the book b) the class number c) the publisher	whether the book contains a chapter on *illustrations* (*YES/NO*)
a book entitled *A Dictionary of Biological Terms* (or similar)	a) the place of publication b) its location in the library c) the number of pages it contains d) the class number	the meaning of the term *lagopodous*
any book on the subject of *energy conservation*	a) the author b) the title c) the date of publication d) the class number	whether the book contains information on a) electric cars (*YES/NO*) b) domestic solar heating (*YES/NO*)
any book about FORTRAN programming	a) the title b) the publisher c) its location in the library d) the class number	whether the book explains *Simpson's Rule* (*YES/NO*)

a book entitled *Personnel Management* (or similar)	a) the exact title b) the author c) the date of publication d) the class number	the number of the chapter that contains information about the *orientation of new employees*
any book by *Samuelson* that might be used by students of Economics, Management, or Business Studies	a) the class number b) the title c) the date of publication d) the number of pages it contains	whether the book contains a) a glossary b) an index
any book about *environmental pollution as a result of technological advances*	a) the title b) the author c) the place of publication d) the class number	whether the book contains information about the effects of industrial noise on workers' health. (*YES/NO*)
a book entitled *Production Management* (or similar)	a) the author b) the class number c) the date of publication	whether the book contains sections on: a) research and development (*YES/NO*) b) patents (*YES/NO*) c) plant layout (*YES/NO*)
a book entitled *Organic Chemistry* (or similar)	a) the exact title b) the class number c) the publisher d) the author	how many pages are devoted to the *molecular structure of carbohydrates*
A book entitled *Vector Mechanics for Engineers* (or similar)	a) the class number b) the author c) the publisher d) the date of publication	whether the book explains how *forced vibrations of a system* occur